P9-BYT-869

The WILD GARDENER

On Flowers and Foliage for the Natural Border

PETER LOEWER

STACKPOLE
BOOKS

Copyright © 1991 by Peter Loewer

Published by
STACKPOLE BOOKS
Cameron and Kelker Streets
P.O. Box 1831
Harrisburg, PA 17105

All rights reserved, including the right to reproduce this book or portions thereof in any form or by any means, electronic or mechanical, including photocopying, recording, or by any information storage and retrieval system, without permission in writing from the publisher. All inquiries should be addressed to Stackpole Books, Cameron and Kelker Streets, P.O. Box 1831, Harrisburg, Pennsylvania 17105.

Printed in the United States of America

First Edition

10 9 8 7 6 5 4 3 2

Cover art and interior illustrations by Peter Loewer.

To Jean

Library of Congress Cataloging-in-Publication Data

Loewer, H. Peter.
    The wild gardener : on flowers and foliage for the natural border
  / Peter Loewer. – 1st ed.
        p.   cm.
    Includes index.
    ISBN 0-8117-0885-3 (HC) : $19.95 ($26.95 Can.)
    1. Wild flower gardening–United States. 2. Native plant
gardening–United States. 3. Wild flowers–United States.
4. Native plants for cultivation–United States. 5. Wild flowers–
Folklore. I. Title.
SB439.L64 1991
635.9'676'0973–dc20   91-15394
                                                                                                         CIP

CONTENTS

Acknowledgments
vii

Introduction
1

Acknowledgments

Except perhaps for the autobiography of St. Simon Stylites, no one ever sits down and singlehandedly writes a book. First the present author must credit the authors of the past. In this case, they include, among others, Mrs. William Starr Dana, Neltje Blanchan, Henry David Thoreau, Britton and Brown, Liberty Hyde Baily, Harold William Rickett, and many American poets of the past 250 years.

Then there are those who provide inspiration, like Bebe Miles, who first taught me the importance of wildflowers in the scheme of things, and author-illustrators such as Roger Tory Peterson, who made the field guides so accessible and popular.

Thanks must go to the *Sullivan County Democrat* for printing my weekly column that began as "The Catskill Gardener," changed to "The Mountain Gardener," and runs today as "Back to the Garden"; many of the shorter pieces first appeared there. And a tip of the gardener's hat to the editors of *The American Horticulturist* for publishing the articles on the spiders and butterflies, and *Kaatskill Life* for printing some of the longer wildflower essays.

Finally there are the friends and associates of the present: Dominick Able, my agent, for his continued support; Sally Atwater, my editor at Stackpole Books, for her intelligence at editing and for suggesting what all who know me call the perfect title; Ben Wechsler, for continuing to fight for protecting and saving the land; Budd Myers for wildflowers in the rock garden; Janet Gracey for her wild garden and the many happy hours spent with weekend wildflowers; Frank and Marge Martin for making a lot of this book possible; and my wife, Jean, for so many things there is no room for the tally.

INTRODUCTION

My first experience with wildflowers was roaming the spring countryside around Buffalo, New York, with my parents and my younger brother, David. After a winter on the edge of Lake Erie, the mere suggestion of traipsing about a woods where the floor was carpeted with hepaticas and violets pushing up through the snow-worn leaves was enough to warm the coldest chambers of our hearts. And these wildflowers not only bloomed before their civilized cousins in my mother's garden—they were distinctly different, being smaller, almost elfin, and quite refined in both color and form.

Soon I found a wonderful old book to help us in our search. *How to Know the Wild Flowers,* by Mrs. William Starr Dana, originally published in 1895, was found in a used bookstore in Buffalo, after it had been deassessioned by the Library Company of Philadelphia in 1949. Within its creamy, acid-free pages were descriptions of 164 American native plants and charming pen-and-ink drawings to accompany each.

The following quote by Richard Jefferies graced the title page:

> The first conscious thought about wild flowers was to find out their names—the first conscious pleasure—and then I began to see so many that I had not previously noted. Once you wish to identify them, there is nothing escapes, down to the little white chickweed of the path and the moss of the wall.

Years passed and false careers came and went, and I became a writer who chose to write about gardens, plants, and nature.

Eventually I established two woodland gardens devoted only to American wildflowers: The first lasted twenty years and encompassed some thirty acres, forty-five miles from civilization; the present wild garden is and will be part of one acre, three and a half miles from city hall.

ABOUT THE LAND

The larger garden was in the Catskill Mountains of New York State at an elevation of thirteen hundred feet. The USDA lists that area as Zone 5a with a minimum winter temperature of − 20°F. But every few winters we hit a low of − 30°F, often accompanied by thirty-mile-an-hour winds – and sometimes with no snow cover at all – yet the gardens survived.

The land was mostly old farmland that had once been cleared and allowed to return to nature, plus some land that had been leveled to put up tourist houses and a hotel.

To reclaim the land we carted away a half-century of junk including elixir bottles, blue bromo bottles, wire coat hangers, light bulbs, enamel pans with rusted bottoms, Kendal oil cans, and dozens – no, hundreds – of glass fuses. After a few years of trying, I knew there was no chance of having an English border, not where summer storms would topple trees, and winter winds could easily tear the gutters off old frame houses.

And the land was not that good. A very thin layer of topsoil lay over a few feet of red shale and heavy clay. But we would dig and turn and turn and dig, bringing bags of composted cow and sheep manure from the local ag store and bushels of leaf litter from the woods. And slowly the soil improved.

Some years we had a surfeit of rain: Inch after inch would fall. I would go out and implore Minerva, the rain goddess, to stop – but the clouds would only thicken and the rains of Ranchipur continue to fall. But the gardens survived.

Not surprisingly, the plants that grew the best were the native Americans and some tough old Europeans: the violets, the daylilies, the white pines, and the goldenrods, the hops, the nettles, the trilliums–and the gardens grew bigger.

Then we moved to a warmer climate–a climate whose summers were just as oppressive but whose winters were appreciatively milder–for a very simple reason: More plants would grow and more wild plants lived in the mountains around us.

The new garden is only an acre, but what an acre: water, rocks, walls, good soil, bad soil, an old house that still needs a lot of work–and a new place to garden.

About the Temperature Zones

The United States Department of Agriculture issued a new USDA Plant Hardiness Zone Map in January 1990. Average annual minimum temperatures on the new map have been based on the lowest temperatures recorded for each of the years 1974 to 1986 in the United States and Canada. A new Zone 11, where temperatures are 40°F and above, has been added.

Even now there is some controversy over the accuracy of using a one-time low temperature to change the averages of an entire zone. And it will be years before nurseries and catalogs adopt the new map, even longer for most books to reflect any changes. This book uses the map revised in 1965.

America's Most Popular Wildflowers–in 1949

Harold N. Moldenke, curator and administrator of the herbarium at the New York Botanical Garden, wrote *American Wild Flowers.* The flowers he chose were limited to herbaceous flowering plants occurring without cultivation in the United States, Canada, Newfoundland, Alaska, Greenland, St. Pierre, and Miquelon (these last two are islands belonging to France, just off the coast of Newfoundland)–more than seven million square miles. He had asked a thousand naturalists and botanists

to list the twelve showiest, most conspicuous, and most interesting wildflowers likely to be seen by lovers of nature. He
sifted through the returns with nominations for more than a
thousand plants and tallied the votes for the top fifteen:

  1. Cardinal flower *(Lobelia cardinalis)*   213
  2. Showy ladyslipper *(Cypripedium reginae)*   155
  3. New England aster *(Aster novae-angliae)*   145
  4. Butterflyweed *(Asclepias tuberosa)*   141
  5. Moccasinflower *(Cypripedium acaule)*   136
  6. White wakerobin *(Trillium grandiflorum)*   134
  7. Wild columbine *(Aquilegia canadensis)*   131
  8. Sweet-scented white waterlily *(Nymphaea odorata)*   109
  9. Eastern fringed gentian *(Gentianopsis crinata)*   107
 10. Common marsh marigold *(Caltha palustris)*   88
 11. Black-eyed Susan *(Rudbeckia hirta)*   80
 12. Bloodroot *(Sanguinaria canadensis)*   79
 13. Larger blueflag *(Iris versicolor)*   77
 14. Virginia bluebell *(Mertensia virginica)*   77
 15. Turk's-cap lily *(Lilium superbum)*   67

Of those fifteen plants, eleven have always been in our
gardens and are included in this book.

As for the other four, the showy ladyslipper requires a cool,
moist, woodsy soil, and I never got around to site preparation
or finding a source. The eastern fringed gentian was represented in our wild garden by the closed gentian, but I suspect
I'll start a plant next year. The larger blueflag is a perfect plant
for the margins of lakes or ponds but still awaits introduction
to our water gardens. The Virginia bluebell, though a perfectly
beautiful flower, shifts into dormancy by June, and I've yet to
find the perfect spot for such a plant.

The point about wildflowers from 1949 is that now, some
forty years later, it seems that the pendulum has swung away

from cookie-cutter floral displays and the kind of garden that only retired wealthy stockbrokers or movie stars have; it is swinging back to the wild end of the garden.

ABOUT LATIN

I have a friend in the Men's Garden Club who took Latin in high school. Since he has worked in horticulture most of his adult life, Bernie Grass is delighted that he did. But, he admits, he did write the following when forced to attend his first class in Latin:

All the Romans dead who spoke it;
All the people dead who wrote it;
All the students die who learn it;
Blessed death—and they deserve it!

Throughout this book I have used the botanical names for plants, names that are in Latin or Greek. To make it more interesting, I have given the meanings of the words and the reasons those particular words were chosen. There is a movement in the garden world, a movement based upon the notion that the American public is too shallow to care about such words. A number of magazines and newspapers, including publications that should know better, have decided not to use them in order to keep the readership up. I know they are wrong.

Latin names are used in this book because with so many common names, with so many plants, in a country so large, there are bound to be duplications. The only way to get the plant you want is to use the proper name.

RAPING THE WILD

If a nursery offers you wildflowers for $2.95, wildflowers that you know take five or six years to mature from seedlings, something is wrong. If a plant is listed as endangered and someone offers you three or four—"Pssst! Buddy! Have I got a deal for you!"—please look the other way. Don't encourage them. By the time a plant is put on the endangered list, it's usually too late to save it.

If you find an endangered plant on property that is not your own, do not take it. The only time you have the right to remove such a plant is when the steam shovel is waiting in the wings and the bulldozer is rumbling at your heels. Then make an honest effort to find the owner before you begin digging.

THE WILD END OF THE GARDEN

One of the five books I would rush to save if the house caught on fire is called *Corners of Grey Old Gardens*. It's an English collection of gardening essays edited by Margaret Waterfield, published in 1917, and deassessioned by the Cleveland Garden Center; I found in a used-book store in Manhattan for $2. In "The Joy of Gardens," Richard Le Gallienne writes of the home end and the wild end of the garden. I wish I had thought of it first:

> Man went forth to his labour until the evening, and now it is evening; and the prayer of his thanks-giving sends a happy murmur up to the evening sky. Such are the sounds at the home end of the garden.
>
> Then you wander towards the wild end of the garden, and the light seems to grow spectral, and the air haunted. Here are no warm windows or friendly human behavior, only whispering gleams and beck-onings and half-frightened sounds calling you out, calling you away, calling you beyond.

THE FIRST FLOWER OF SPRING

Coltsfoot — *Tussilago farfara*

In our area of the mountains, the back roads become icy from a combination of melting snow, sleet and rainstorms in March, and persistent mud. Ruts are made by city folk, the men and women we call weekend warriors, who drive trucks with tires that could eat Chicago. They come up to the mountains to prove philosophies: For the men, it's virility and lost manhood; the women, in extension of the fight for rights conducted all week long in New York, seek an entry into the world of the Amazons.

The ditches on either side of the ruts are full of sand dropped for years by the trucks of the town highway department, the sand cut with calcium chloride to prevent initial freezing. (For years, salt and sand were stored in a pile at the town garage, but after salting the well water for the town hall, they changed to a less destructive formula.)

These visitors have no idea that a world of wild things exists in the woods that begin on either side of the ditches. During hunting season, all the leafless trees stand stark and bare, relieved only by the green of a few conifers. Under the snow the wildflowers are safely dormant for the winter; the animals are in their burrows and the birds are in the suburbs where the food is good.

In late February to early March, two flowers bloom in the mountains. In the dark recesses of the awakening woods, the skunk cabbages push their way through the worn-out snows. And on top of those now-full ditches, the coltsfoot appear.

The blossoms would probably be less noticeable in May, but in the gray and black of very early spring, the bright yellow sunbursts of these daisylike flowers appear to be piles of golden coins left by the roadside, without the help of a rainbow. Many slender rays make a disk on top of a reddish stalk that bears a few scales. There are no leaves, for these appear later in the year after the potential for heavy frosts and snows are past, often not until the end of April.

Coltsfoot is an alien brought to America by the colonists as a folk remedy. The genus name, *Tussilago,* is from *tussis,* "to cough," and refers to the medicinal use of the leaves. There is only one species, *farfara,* a name taken from *folia farfarae,* the apothecary's name for the cough preparation made from the leaves.

For centuries, the dried leaves (stems removed) were mixed with other herbs – chiefly thyme, rosemary, horehound, marshmallow, and chamomile – then used as a pipe tobacco, or made into cigarettes, and smoked to relieve coughs and asthma.

The early Romans burned the leaves and roots over charcoal and then inhaled the smoke through hollow reeds. In Pliny's day, they swallowed wine between puffs.

Contemporary research suggests that the heavy sap might help reduce the swelling of mucous membranes but doctors also warn that too much is potentially dangerous to the liver.

Although coltsfoot flowers have been used in folk medicine – usually in teas – it is the leaf that is most important. These are slightly lobed, toothed, and up to eight inches wide. In the days of the flintlock rifle, the down from the underside of the leaves was used as tinder. Birds employ the fluff to line their nests.

Like most interlopers, this is a tough plant. Witness the dirt it lives in: a combination of road salts, sand, pure clay, and rock. And coltsfoot is invasive, with each bit of root able to produce more of its own kind. So it's best left to the wild garden, planted at the edge of a woods where it will get partial shade in summer and can be kept in check by a weed wacker or lawn mower. But when it is established in the woodland, spring visitors will be charmed first by the flowers, and later in the year by the luxurious growth of the leaves.

THOREAU'S CUP

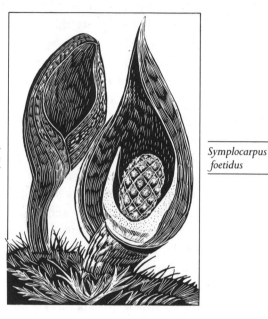

Skunk cabbage

Symplocarpus foetidus

It's a misty morning in late March. The woods is awash with wet. Underfoot, the forest duff is about as soaked as duff can get, yet I walk along in comfort, wearing my rubber boots and a pair of thick wool socks. *Duff,* by the by, is one of those wonderful words that have not only a touch of the strange but a recognizable history as well. It's a Scottish word, originally used to describe the soft and spongy feel of pressing into a loaf of fresh bread or a turnip past its prime. It could also be described, onomatopoeically, as the sound made by striking a soft, spongy substance, much as when a beaver thwacks the water with its tail. From those beginnings, it came to mean the decaying vegetable matter found on the forest floor. As the author of the

1886 report of the forest commission of New York State noted: "I have seen the smoke from fires in the duff even after the snow has fallen."

There are few sounds outside the squish produced by my own passing and the continuous drip from water that accumulates on the burgeoning buds dotting the shiny, black branches overhead. The mist also accumulates, forming tiny beads that swell until they reach the size that makes them fall to the ground below. My boots are now quite slick, and as I pass through dips in the trail, my glasses become glazed with fog. From the trees that line a farmer's field a half-mile away, I can hear the cawing of a few crows.

The caws from the black crows and the word *duff* and its Scottish origins, in combination with the wet and barren branches, suggest the gallant Macduff. In turn, my mind's eye transforms some of the twisted trees and stumps in the swamp just ahead of me into the silhouette of the witches three, those beauties who cavort in the prologue of *Macbeth;* then as I draw nearer, my imagination cools.

As I reach the edge of the water—part of which is still crusted with ice from last night's cold—I look about and see one old and mossed hemlock stump, its beveled but lichened surface giving evidence of a decapitation that must have occurred years ago. There between the gnarled base of the stump and a pile of last autumn's needles and leaves, I see a group of plump and short, purple-mottled, shell-like leaves, each wearing a monk's cowl crowned with curls that resemble chocolate shaved for the top of a fancy cake.

These are the flowers of the skunk cabbage. Its botanical name is *Symplocarpus foetidus.* The genus name comes from *symploke*, "connection," and *karpos*, "fruit," referring to the ovaries consolidating into a single fruit. Like the calla lily (that symbol of the sophistication of the 1930s), the flamingo flower of house plant fame, and the jack-in-the-pulpit, the skunk cabbages belong to the family of plants known as the arums, and all bear flowers quite alike in structure.

Each round and curling leaf–more properly termed a spathe–is just a raincoat for the flowers within. The tiny blossoms encircle a stiff projection called a spadix. If you pry apart the flaps of the cowl, you will see tiny golden dots that twine around a central totem, the spadix.

In the marshy duff where the skunk cabbage blooms, there also live many tiny flies and gnats that awaken to the spring about the same time as the flowers do. They can easily pass through the tentlike openings in each spathe to reach the drops of nectar produced by the little flowers within, and so pollination is assured. But every so often a honeybee, chancing to pass through the late March or April woods–for some years the cabbage may bloom later than others–will spy the spathe and fly down to sample the nectar within. (One does wonder what bee, what member of that insect society whose genetic memory is programed for flowers both glorious and bright would be tempted by something that could pass for a tiny, purplish yurt housing gnats and forest beetles.)

Once inside, bees and larger visitors are often trapped because, although they can push their way in, the opening is often too small for their escape. This, of course, is not purposeful, because honeybees, like many Americans, are immigrants and were not around for the skunk cabbage to consider when its design was formulated.

Now as to its name: Rumor has it that this plant produces a prodigious scent, often strong enough to endow the surrounding landscape with an overpowering odor of dread. No, indeed. That's just not so. It's a definite maligning of the skunk. The odor from bruised leaves is not particularly fetching but certainly is never enough to prevent one's enjoyment of the woods in early spring.

There are thirty-nine entries in Thoreau's journals for skunk cabbage, so I know that my liking for this first flower of spring puts me in good company. Thoreau wrote,

> I see in the swamps under the cliff the dark decaying leaves of the skunk cabbage, four or five spreading every way so flat and decayed as to look like a fungus or mildew, making it doubtful at first what plant it is; but there is the sharp green bud already revealed in the centre between the leaf stalks, ready to expand in the spring.

And it's true. The flowers are actually formed underground in the autumn, and the whole affair – spathe, spadix, and budding flowers – pushes up early the following spring, generating enough heat in rapid growth to thaw the soil around it, often rising up through snow and ice.

After the spathe withers, the leaves appear, often reaching a length of three feet. A skunk cabbage leaf, writes Thoreau,

> makes the best vessel to drink out of at a spring, it is so large, already somewhat dishing, oftenest entire, and grows near at hand, and though its odor when the stem is cut off is offensive, it does not flavor the water and is not perceived in drinking.

For those gardeners who have a sizable bog garden, these plants make wonderful additions, for their leaves are a vivid green and are large enough to color the world about them.

As for using these leaves when drinking from a spring, I am reminded that Thoreau eventually left Walden for a pencil factory, and so I recommend using a cup.

GOOD TIMES UNDERGROUND

Meadow vole — *Microtus pennsylvanicus*

Eastern mole — *Scalopus aquaticus*

Some years, when the snows of winter have melted, you may hear loud cries of despair echoing from hill to hill as home-owners survey their backyards and suddenly become aware that their once-even lawns are now traversed with tunnels dug by moles—along with an occasional shrew. What was a swath of peaceful green now resembles the B&O rail yards.

The worst mole years tend to follow summers that feature bumper crops of grubs, especially Japanese beetles. Moles are little mammals with tiny eyes, small concealed ears, and very pretty, soft iridescent fur. They live almost entirely under-ground, feeding on smaller animal life, especially earthworms and grubs. I emphasize: Moles do not eat bulbs or roots. They will chew through them if the plants are in the way, but they do not ingest the results of their chewing. They are generally beneficial to gardens, especially when it comes to consuming vast numbers of voracious grubs. I do admit that, in their zeal to devour, moles often do some damage by heaving up the soil, causing the grass to dry out quickly and creating unsightly ridges or tunnel-tops—a sight that irritates some people more than paying taxes.

Now there are methods used to remove moles. Cyanide gas, for example, is dangerous to both the mole and the man. And hooking up a hose to the exhaust of a car is messy to the lawn and dangerous to everybody. But outside of these, nothing is sure.

Catalogs sell windmills featuring spikes in the ground that supposedly make a rumbling noise in the earth, scaring away moles. But I've never seen it work; they still dig tunnels and hunt for food but perhaps move out of the area only to dine.

Recently, a garden writer told me of putting in the tunnels either a dead mole or a hunk of odiferous cheese. But he has no proof that either works. And there was no hint given on how to obtain a dead mole to begin with, although steel traps are also offered for sale by some catalogs.

Poison bait isn't such a good idea, especially if you have a cat, dog, or child that you value. But there is an effective biological control called milky spore disease; it inoculates your soil with a fungal disease that infects the grubs but bothers nothing else. The problem with this product is the time it takes to effect the cure—at least a year.

So before going out and putting a toxic waste dump in your backyard to do away with the little pests or driving up the family car to gas them out, think ahead to next July and the damage done by the beetles to the garden and the favors the moles have done for you. Remember that the number of moles is in direct proportion to the food supply, and if your backyard and garden have a surfeit of moles, they probably need them.

Instead, buy a pair of those plastic shoes with spikes used to aerate the lawn (not, as some think, to kill the moles) and walk over those tunnels. Then plant some grass seed, rake it up a bit, and by mid-May you'll never know they were there.

And then there are voles. One spring, after the last of the snows had melted, I went out into the garden to check on the damages wrought by the weeks of ice and chill and bitter blasts. What a disaster! Plants that had lived through the past five winters had given up the leaf. But by far the worst damage was perpetrated by our little furry friend, the vole. Everywhere I turned, the ground, the hay mulches, the backyard lawn, and piles of leaves were tunneled through and through. Where grasses touched the trunks of small trees and bushes like my arctic willow or my Himalayan honeysuckle, the bark was chewed unmercifully. My entire line of lavender was eaten right down to soil level, and—blast them—they had taken all the leaves of the lambs tongue and ripped them up for nesting material.

The *Complete Guide to American Wildlife* has this to say about the vole:

> Voles are best known to many readers by the popular name of "meadow mice." Voles have long, grayish brown fur, short ears and tails, and beady eyes. Their tails are more than an inch long, and are not brightly colored. They live on the ground usually in grassy terrain, where they make inch-wide runways, leaving behind cut grass stems, and are active at all hours. They can swim and dive. In winter they make round holes to the surface through the snow.

Their voice is a high-pitched squeak. They eat grass, roots, bark, and seeds. They construct a nest of plant material on the ground, and there are usually 5–7 young.

The vole that did the damage to our gardens this year is known as *Microtus pennsylvanicus,* the meadow vole. This vole is between three and five inches long with an average two-inch tail and was known as Danny Meadow Mouse in the *Burgess Bedtime Stories.* A population of 15 to an acre can increase to 250 voles in four years. Obviously, that kind of growth explosion had occurred in the land about our home.

Our garden cat, Miss Jekyll, had tried to do her bit with the vole menace: Every afternoon, a freshly killed subject showed up on the doormat in front of the back door. I'm sure she had dispatched many more out in the garden and the fields beyond.

But that same spring, the snowdrops were truly beautiful, and the crocuses the best ever. And by mid-May, the few remaining vole tunnels were a faint remembrance of things past.

THE HUMBLE BUMBLE

Rock lichen

Lecidea speirea

Bumblebee

Bombus pennsylvanicus

Hair-cap moss

Polytrichum commune

Burly, dozing humble-bee
Where thou art is clime for me.
Let them sail for Porto Rique,
Far-off heats through seas to seek;
I will follow thee alone,
Thou animated torrid-zone!

Emerson knew of what he wrote when he penned the poem above. Animated torrid-zone – what better name for this furry blimp that buzzes around the garden?

Of course you can ask, Why is the bumblebee so important? Because before the seventeenth century, all the trees and flowers of America were pollinated by our native insects, including the various kinds of bumblebee. The true honeybee *(Apis mellifera)* was not found in North or South America until the settlers arrived with their hives in tow.

That's right. The ubiquitous honeybee is a relatively new immigrant, right along with the gypsy moth, the Japanese beetle, the Mediterranean fruit fly, and all those giant frogs of Florida.

There are a number of species in the bumblebee genus of the Tribe Bombini. The golden northern bumblebee *(Bombus fervidus)* ranges from Quebec and New Brunswick south to Georgia, then west to California, and north to British Columbia. There is a black band between the wings, and the body is yellow near the wings and black to the rear. The workers are about three quarters of an inch long, and the queen measures almost one inch.

The golden-orange bumblebee *(Bombus borealis)* is about the same size but is orange-yellow and has more black where the legs meet the body.

The larger American bumblebee *(Bombus pennsylvanicus)* ranges throughout the United States and Canada. It is black behind the wings, then yellow, then black again.

Like the honeybees, bumblebees are social creatures. But unlike their smaller relatives, each one can sting many times if provoked. But, I hasten to add, they are difficult to anger, and unless you wave about and slap at them, as far as they are concerned, you are nothing except a large tree with colored leaves and no threat at all.

The bumblebee story begins in spring with a single bee, a queen, who has mated the previous autumn and has yet to lay any eggs. With the blooming of the coltsfoot *(Tussilago farfara)* along the back roads, and crocus and snowdrops in the garden, the first queen bumblebees leave their winter quarters where they have rested for some six months.

A bee's first duty is food, for she's weak and lethargic after her hibernation. You may often find a queen basking in the spring sunshine atop a lichened fieldstone, hardly moving but obviously alive to the sun's heat and quietly storing energy as though she is quite unaware of the responsibility she has for the future history of her race. At night and when the weather turns cold, she takes shelter under leaves or in the soil, becoming torpid but awakening when the weather again warms up.

This extended period of rest and relaxation continues for a few weeks while she builds up her strength and the burgeoning spring produces more flowers for her food and the sun warms the earth.

All bumblebees make their homes in the abandoned nests of field mice, voles, and shrews, nests that consist of accumulations of fine pieces of moss, leaves, grass, and other material collected by the former tenants. Here the imagination–tinged, I admit, by childhood memories of Beatrix Potter–envisions little rooms with sloping ceilings and rounded corners heaped with tiny Turkish pillows and hanging with silken tassels like a Victorian cozy corner. The mouse or vole family has departed for somewhere else–a sign that the great American wanderlust has penetrated to the smallest members of the animal kingdom–but has left behind enough creature comforts for the entering bumblebee. The mind's eye can see this furry soul slowly walking from room to room, looking for the perfect place to hang her metaphorical hat and create her share of the summer's population.

Once she has settled in, she begins to lay eggs. Then she builds a wax honey pot just inside the entrance of the nest and uses it to store some of the nectar she has collected in the field. It will be three quarters of an inch high and half an inch in diameter. This is for those blustery or rainy mountain days when she cannot leave home for food.

When the eggs hatch, the queen is forced to feed not only

herself but also her brood, and this she does with a mixture of honey and pollen.

Soon the young bees grow and become workers, who in turn will help the queen look after the welfare of the colony. The queen can then turn her attention to laying more eggs.

Outside in the garden, the flowers bloom and bloom, and bumblebee after bumblebee drones on in the constant search for nectar. The colony grows. And in the words of Emerson,

> *Wiser far than human seer,*
> *Yellow-breeched philospher!*
> *Seeing only what is fair,*
> *Sipping only what is sweet,*
> *Thou dost mock at fate and care,*
> *Leave the chaff, and take the wheat.*

BACK-ROAD RESCUES

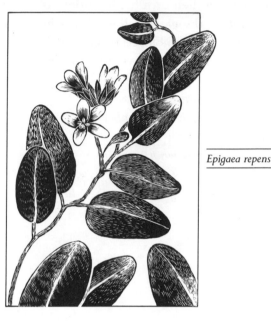

Trailing arbutus

Epigaea repens

In mid-April, our county road crew came through one of the lesser back roads with their "grade-all," a machine of great complexity designed to move (or scrape) large amounts of dirt from one spot to another. They went to work deepening the ditches and, at the same time, sliced all the vegetation on the banks above the road. Early one afternoon, they quit just before reaching a stand of trailing arbutus, *Epigaea repens,* a most beautiful wildflower, long awarded the protected status given to rare and endangered plants.

I returned to the site with basket and trowel and, as carefully as possible, dug up one of the largest bunches. Taking plenty of soil—and painstakingly wrapping the plants in damp newspapers—I hurried to our garden.

There on a bank beneath a white pine, ferns, and some species *rhododendron,* I replanted the arbutus. The buds on the plants were only a few short days away from blooming when I completed the job. The tough, rounded evergreen leaves gave promise of becoming a fine groundcover.

The genus *Epigaea* means "on the earth," and *repens* is the Latin for "creeping," referring to the habit of this plant. When the settlers first arrived, they called them mayflowers, supposedly because they found them blooming in May. But this plant is one of the first flowers of spring, and May is much too late. Probably the name is in honor of their ship.

The arbutus in England is an entirely different plant. They speak of the late-flowering strawberry tree *(Arbutus unedo),* an evergreen shrub with white flowers and rough red berries, with *arbutus* here referring to the fruit.

Many eastern wildflower enthusiasts gauge success by whether they can grow trailing arbutus in their gardens. Arbutus does not travel well and rarely survives transplanting. Neltje Blanchan writes,

> There is little use trying to coax this shyest of sylvan flowers into our gardens where other members of its family, rhododendrons, laurels, and azaleas make themselves delightfully at home. It is wild as a hawk, an untamable creature that slowly pines to death when brought into contact with civilization.

The problem is the acid content of the soil. Without sufficient acidity, the arbutus will surely fail. But the plants also need a spot with excellent drainage in partial sun, yet the ground must be moist, especially with summer heat. This is especially important during the first year: Never let the roots dry out.

If not sure about your soil, test it with a pH tape or take a sample to the local extension service. Arbutus must have a pH of 4.5 to prosper.

Mine failed. Shortly after flowering, the leaves slowly turned brown about the edges, rather like the vanilla wafers made by Nabisco, and before the summer was over, the plants appeared dead.

But two springs later I spied a touch of light pink in the spot where the arbutus once bloomed, and sure enough, one plant survived. Within days I had a few blossoms to entertain our eyes and our noses, and a few early bees. This marvel in no way reflects on my skill. It merely means that the acidity—usually a problem in many Catskill gardens—has acted on my behalf. The soil registers a perfect pH of 4.5.

If you want to try arbutus, buy it only from nurseries that guarantee in-house propagation. Then, after planting it with all the requirements listed above, mulch it with pine needles. Never let it suffer from dryness until it's well established.

RUN! NIMITTI!

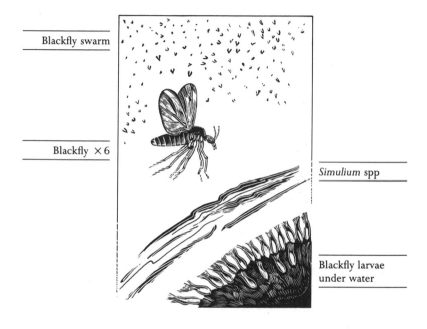

Blackfly swarm

Blackfly ×6

Simulium spp

Blackfly larvae under water

Every spring when the late snows are over, the high winds that break tree limbs subside, the rains that rival those of Ranchipur cease, and the water doesn't freeze in the birdbath every night, we gardeners go out into the garden to garden. Usually, whatever day we choose turns out to be rather dismal. But it gives us a chance to putter about in the muck and think about that day soon to come that the weather forecaster will, in the nightly recap, call one of the year's ten best.

In most of Canada, in the great Northeast, down to Georgia, west to California, and north to Alaska, that fabled day—usually the end of April and the beginning of May—dawns with a glory not seen since the previous fall. We don our boots, take up spades and shovels, grasp our sturdy rakes, unwind the hose, and go out into the sunshine. Within seconds, the blackflies descend — or rise, as the case may be — and begin to gnaw upon our bodies in a way reminiscent of *The Night of the Living Dead.*

They are hungry. With a sensitivity that rivals any available to man, the female flies aim for the nearest exposed skin — arm, ankle, wrist, and nose, even the tender tip of an ear will do. Whereupon they draw blood.

For blackflies are aquatic flies that bite. They are not at all like typical pond dwellers: mayflies that look like bobbing bits of gossamer or sparkling dragonflies that zip across the waters. Instead, they are small, compact, with short broad wings . . . and the females suck blood.

These pests belong to the family Simuliidae. They are called turkey-gnats because one species transmits a blood parasite among turkeys; another does the same for young ducks. But it is chiefly as pests of man and his domestic animals that Simuliidae are important.

According to Harold Oldroyd in his fascinating book *The Natural History of Flies,* an extreme instance of the damage done by these flying drills is in the oft-quoted census made in Romania, Bulgaria, and Yugoslavia in 1923, when nearly twenty thousand domestic animals were said to have been killed by the Golubatz fly, *Simulium columbaschense.* Photographs of men wearing masses of smoldering rope to give a protective smoke from the nimitti, as they called them, made all the newspapers. A newspaper reported, "A few people have been known to remain indoors for several weeks on end during a bad nimitti season."

Blackflies are persistent in their attacks and surround their victims in a milling cloud, often making a flyline for that bit of exposed flesh between pants and socks. Soon, anything exposed is covered with spots of blood from the bites. But remember that half of those specks darting for your hairline are males just along to watch the ladies work.

Blackfly larvae are entirely aquatic. Although it would be pleasant to believe they would need foul water for life support, in truth they will live only in clean water, where they filter tiny bits of plant and animal matter from the currents with efficient mouth brushes, while their posteriors are cemented to rocks and aquatic vegetation.

When it is time, the larvae weave silken cocoons. Within days, the adults emerge from these tiny sleeping bags, which upon opening become distended with air bubbles. Thus, if blackflies happen to be under water when they hatch, they will rise to the surface in a glistening bubble of air and be able to fly away on the attack without even waiting for their bodies to harden, as must other insects.

But soon the horrors of May will pass, and we can once more go into the garden – to face the slugs and Japanese beetles.

A FLEETING FLOWER

Bloodroot

Sanguinaria canadensis

Few things of any great import last for a long time, a case in point being bloodroot. The flowers come and go within a week's time, especially if ravaged by late April or early May winds and rain.

As buds, the perfectly .white blossoms leave the ground wrapped in lobed and rounded leaves, much like a diva emerging into the limelight, dressed in a mantle of silver-green. Then in a burst of early sun, they open to reveal a crowd of golden stamens surrounded by eight to twelve petals about an inch and a half across on six-inch stems.

The flowers produce no nectar, so the bees that pollinate

them are rewarded only with a dusting of pollen in return for stopping by. Before the honeybees came to America, the flowers were serviced by the small Halictid, or mining, bees; a bumblebee landing on this flower would be tantamount to an elephant stepping on a Ping-Pong table. By nightfall, the petals have closed up to protect the pollen for the next day's visitors.

Alice Morse Earle, in *Old Time Gardens*, wrote of the bloodroot:

> In childhood I absolutely abhorred bloodroot; it seemed to me a fearsome thing when first I picked it. I remember well my dismay, it was so pure, so sleek, so innocent of face, yet bleeding at a touch, like a murdered man in the Blood Ordeal.

The genus *Sanguinaria* is from the Latin word for blood, *sanguis* (whence the English word *sanguineous*, used in such marvelous lines as Thackeray's "the sanguineous histories of queens"). The species name is *canadensis*, for the first specimen described was observed in Canada.

The root of this plant is thick, gnarled, and several inches long. Blood red when sliced apart, it bleeds with bright orange-red juice. American Indians used these roots to treat many diseases, including rheumatism and asthma. The juice was also used as a skin decoration both for ceremonies and for war. Today the juice is being examined for use as an antiseptic and is found in health food toothpastes advertised as a plaque inhibitor. Neltje Blanchan mentions its use by colonial mothers who would put a few drops on a sugar lump and give it to children for coughs and colds. However, the authors of *Medicinal Plants* caution against its use because of possible medical complications and the risk of causing tunnel vision.

For the fleeting part of the wild garden, grow bloodroot,

using good humusy, well-drained soil in open shade. Don't pick the flowers, since the petals will quickly fall; let them go to seed instead.

Back in the late 1700s, semidouble forms of bloodroot flowers were found, and today a true double cultivar called – unfortunately – 'Multiplex' is usually available. The blossoms look like small water lilies, and it's one of the few cases when new is as good as old.

Since these doubles are sterile, they last a bit longer in the garden. To propagate, cut the rootstock into a few two-inch pieces and let the wounded surface heal overnight before planting.

WILDFLOWERS
FOR THE WATER

American waterlily   *Nymphaea odorata*

After the pond was finished and that giant scar upon the land
began to fill, the grass seeds that my wife planted all around
began to germinate and root.

Cattails arrived the first year. Their seeds are bits of fluff
that blow with the breeze, and no pond is safe from their
invasions. Arrowheads began to grow in the inlet, and soon
there were minnows, too.

"Where did the fish come from?" folks would ask.

"The birds brought them," I would reply.

"Tell us another," they would say.

"It's true. The birds that wade along the edges of ponds pick up fish eggs on their claws, then fly to our pond, walk around, and soon we have fish."

They would nod their heads as though they believed me, but I knew they didn't.

But wildflowers for the pond—what to pick?

In a marshy area at the far end, the soil would always be wet, and the sun would shine at least half a day before being shaded by the surrounding woods. Here I planted marsh marigold *(Caltha palustris)*. I had been familiar with the plant for years, since it crowded the edges of a woodland pool that I walked by at least once a week.

There in the early spring, not too long after the peepers would start to peep, the tops of mostly sunken logs would frame a rounded rectangle of about twenty square feet with a bubbling pavement of bright yellow-gold as the marsh marigolds would start to bloom.

Their other nicknames include American cowslip, king-cup, May-blob, and souci d'eau. Inch-wide flowers are borne on stems up to two feet high. Their five petals (really sepals) appear waxy yellow, the color of the best butter in the world. The heart-shaped leaves are succulent and were indeed used for salads by the early settlers. *Caltha* is an old name used by Virgil and Pliny for a yellow flower, possibly the true marigold; *palustris* means "in a marsh."

In England the bright yellow primrose *(Primula officinalis)* grows in the middle of fields and marshes, places where cows would wander, making the earth particularly fertile. Hence, *cowslop* became *cowslip,* and American settlers brought the name along when seeing the marsh marigold. Although *souci d'eau* could be literally translated as "worry about the water," it also is the French for water marigold.

This is the kind of flower that is perfect for a wild garden, since it blooms when the days are warm but the nights still chilly, and it's able to resist a late snow, its blaze of gold even more bright against an inch of white. It is content to be green for a month or two. And then, as the weather really heats up and the sun flies high, marsh marigolds become dormant, slowly disappearing, lying in wait for the following year. It can be propagated by division in early spring or by seed.

Cowslips were widely used in colonial days for a cough syrup: A leaf tea was mixed with maple sugar. But gardeners today are warned that the plants are a potential skin irritant and not to be taken internally.

But what about the water proper? I remember the hardy water lilies from childhood visits to the banks of a woodland pond outside Buffalo, New York. The plant was *Nymphaea odorata,* a hardy water lily of very sweet fragrance that bears white or pink double flowers two to four inches across, which stand above round floating leaves up to ten inches across. The genus is named in honor of *nymphe,* a water nymph.

Once again we have a plant that the American Indians used for medicinal purposes, They mixed the roots in a tea for tuberculosis and inflamed glands. In folk medicine a blend of the root and lemon juice was used to remove freckles and pimples.

This flower is superb for a small pond and just as good in a six-inch flowerpot submerged in half a whisky barrel or a child's wading pool—one way to have a water garden while saving the money for the big one.

To grow *Nymphaea* in a clay pot, mix some water lily fertilizer (these plants are hungry) with heavy garden soil, planting the water lily root so that it is covered to the crown. Soak the pot thoroughly, then add a thin layer of small stones or gravel to keep the soil from being disturbed, and gently lower the plant into the pool, keeping about a foot of water above the pot. Until the leaves really begin to grow, put the pot on some bricks so that the water is only a few inches above the crown.

If the pond does not freeze to the level of the water lily, you can leave it outdoors in a northern winter. Otherwise, keep the pots in a cool (not freezing) spot and keep them moist. Set them out again the following spring.

A NATIVE GROUND COVER

Wild ginger

Asarum canadense

cross-section
of seed capsule

There are some seventy-five species of wild gingers, mostly from Japan, but seven or eight are native Americans. Of those, the most important is *Asarum canadense,* a plant that lives in rich woods and various shaded areas from Quebec and New Brunswick to Ontario and Minnesota, then south to North Carolina and Arkansas. *Asarum* is from the Greek *asaron,* the Greek name for a European species long grown for medicinal purposes.

The common name comes from a confusion of herbs. Because the long rootstocks have the taste and odor of the ginger of commerce *(Zingiber officinalis),* early settlers thought that the American roots were a wild variety of the tropical rhizomes from southeast Asia.

American Indians prized wild ginger and used the root to make tea for upset stomachs, coughs, and colds, to reduce fevers, to relieve gas, and to treat cramps. The roots also contain an antitumor compound called aristolochic acid.

The Chippewas would add cut-up pieces of root to flavor food. They treated inflammations by taking equal parts of this and the roots of the common plantain weed *(Plantago major),* spreading the resulting compound on a fresh plantain leaf for use as a poultice.

The *U.S. Pharmacopoeia* (1820–1873) and the *National Formulary* (1916–1947) listed the dried rhizomes of *Asarum canadense,* and in 1961, two antibiotic agents were isolated from chemicals present in the plants.

The flowers bloom in early spring with one flower per plant. Staying close to the ground, they emerge from the earth as button-buds that soon open into single, dull purple-brown, three-part flowers with the shape of a cup. Country children of long ago called them "little brown jugs."

Mrs. William Starr Dana called certain flowers "vegetable cranks." She listed the evening primrose, which opens only at night; the closed gentian, which never opens at all; and the wild ginger, whose odd, unlovely flowers turn their faces to the ground.

No butterfly will trespass here, the pollinators being instead small flies, bugs, or an occasional beetle. These insects crawl from under layers of forest litter, their legs moving sluggishly. Still cold from the slow-melting winter, they take shelter from the night within the flowers.

When a bud opens, the stigma is mature and ready to

receive pollen brought from another, more mature flower. After the stigma withers, twelve stamens emerge and produce pollen to be taken by more low-level fliers to another flower.

This is not a plant to wax eloquent over. But as a ground-cover, the plants are fine, especially appealing in the wild garden or grown on a bank. The broad, dark green leaves are up to seven inches across; their bitter taste encourages rabbits to leave them alone.

The plants like a rich, humusy soil on the acid side in full shade, so they are perfect for growing under shrubs and hedges. Just be sure they never dry out during summers when rains are short.

Unfortunately, wild ginger is not evergreen in northern winters. So gardeners often choose a species found from Virginia and West Virginia south to Georgia and Alabama. Called *Asarum shuttleworthi*, it has heart-shaped leaves that are three inches across and often mottled.

THE WOODS IN MAY

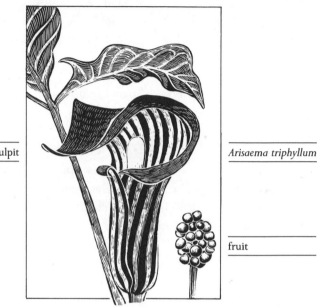

Jack-in-the-pulpit

Arisaema triphyllum

fruit

Often in May, while wandering through the Catskill woods, we would come upon an open glade, an area shaded by the new green leaves above. The surrounding ground was tossed with stones left in an awkward tumble by the glaciers of ten thousand years ago. A mirror of water lay in a rock-lined hole left in the forest floor by the gnarled and entwined roots of a tree that once fell over and took a chunk of earth with it. Sometimes an underground stream ran by, and in the silence of the forest, we could hear the ripple of the waters.

That glistening pool—its bottom carpeted with fallen brown leaves overlaid like playing cards—showed here and there the brilliant vermilion dots of water mites engaged in the hunt.

Close by stood a gathering of one of the most charming wild-flowers of spring, the jack-in-the-pulpit. With luck we would find a dozen or more plants, all in bloom at the same time, so closely placed that their roots were tangled throughout the thin layer of rich, moist earth and the cool, gray surfaces of the rocks. It's no wonder that the "jacks" seem to be at a church convention where they have been allowed to bring their pulpits.

Just as there are differences in preachers, there are differences in pulpits. Sometimes the flowers will be light green, sometimes purple-brown. For years botanists thought the color indicated the sex of the flower. But now we know that every blossom is unisexual, with tiny male and female flowers sharing space at the base of the "jack," or spadix, blooming at different times.

The generic name, *Arisaema*, signifies bloody arum and refers to the red leaves of certain species. But Mrs. William Starr Dana, in her lovely book *How to Know the Wild Flowers*, writes of an old legend that claims the colors were received at the Crucifixion:

> *Beneath the cross it grew;*
> *And in the vase-like hollow of the leaf,*
> *Catching from that dread sower of agony*
> *A few mysterious drops, transmitted thus*
> *Unto the groves and hills their healing stains,*
> *A heritage, for storm or vernal shower*
> *Never to blow away.*

The species name, *triphyllum*, refers to the three leaflets usually overtopping the spathe.

As with much of life today, there are complications with the names of this flower. Many contemporary authorities now recognize three distinct groups: the predominant species, *triphyllum*, with the pulpit green, striped green and purple-brown, or purple-brown throughout; and three subspecies. The first, also called *triphyllum,* has generally asymmetric leaves and pulpits striped green or purple-brown within. A second, termed *pusillum,* has a smaller spathe, is usually all brown or red within, and blooms later than the others. And a third, known as *stewardsonii,* has leaves that are dark green beneath and a spathe with the tube strongly fluted. Naturally, within each group individual flowers strike off on their own in variations of all those mentioned above and more.

The flowers are not fertilized by bees, for these hardy insects are off foraging in the sunlit fields close by. But deep within the woods, the pollination job is assumed by other insects: fungus gnats, flies, and beetles.

Neltje Blanchan writes in *Nature's Garden:*

> A fungus gnat, enticed perhaps by the striped house of refuge from cold spring winds, and with a prospect of food below, enters and slides down the inside walls or the slippery colored column: in either case descent is very easy; it is the return that is made so difficult, if not impossible for the tiny visitor. Squeezing past the projecting ledge [at the base of the spadix] the gnat finds himself in a roomy apartment whose floor—the bottom of the pulpit—is dusted over with fine pollen; that is, if he is among staminate flowers already mature.

Now the pollen-besotted gnat tries to escape. But the walls are too slippery, and its wings keep hitting the projecting ledge above. But if it perseveres, it will find one opening, a gap in the fold of the spathe, and finally escape to the outside. Once free, with the intelligence level of its kind, it will quickly fly to another flower, this time with pollen.

Often visitors are exhausted by the rigors of escape and fall dead to the flower floor, and if you peel open one of Jack's pulpits, you will sometimes find the dead victims.

Fertilized flowers shed the spathe, and by high summer the spadix becomes studded with bright scarlet berries. One of the local names for this flower is memory-root: Students in rural schools years ago were bidden to bite these bitter berries, so as not ever to be tempted again. The Indians, however, would boil the berries along with the tuberous roots to remove the acrid and mouth-burning juices; the pulp was left to dry and then was ground into a meal or used in gruel. Indian turnip, in fact, is another name for the plant.

When it comes to the wild garden, the jack-in-the-pulpit is valuable for many reasons: The flower is attractive, the leaves are pleasant to look at, and the brilliant red berries of fall make a most effective dash of color in the autumn garden.

When planting out, remember to use gloves because some people's skin is irritated by a substance within the bulbs. Choose deep, humusy soil in partial shade, soil that must never dry out. Once these conditions are met, you will have a powerful ally in the garden. Plant in groups so that the masses of flowers and leaves and berries are united in their effect.

THE LOST BELLS
OF OCONEE

Oconee-bells

Shortia galacifolia

Asa Gray (1810–1888) was a botanist, taxonomist, and one of America's great plant explorers. He was a professor of natural history at Harvard and the teacher of many eminent botanists. But above all, by writing articles and textbooks he was responsible for popularizing the study of botany. His *Manual of Botany* was found on the shelves of most identifiers of North American plants.

In 1839 he saw an unnamed plant while examining various dried specimens at the herbarium of André Michaux in Paris.

The leaves and a single fruit were all that were there; the label said it had been collected in "les hautes montagnes de Caroline."

Michaux (1746–1802) had been sent by the French government to establish nurseries in America and to cultivate plants for naturalization in France. He traversed the American continent, writing a book entitled *Flora Boreali-Americana*.

On one of those jaunts he found *Galax urceolata (G. aphylla)*, the only species of galax, or the wandflower. The narrow racemes of tiny white flowers are quite attractive but it's the leaves of this plant that are extensively collected for use in floral decorations.

Dr. Gray returned home and hunted the mountains of North Carolina for the unnamed plant, entirely without success.

Two years later, he described the plant in print and dedicated it to a Kentucky botanist, Dr. Charles W. Short, giving it the name *Shortia galacifolia,* the species meaning "having a leaf like galax." In this way the plant got its first taste of publicity. After that no botanist worth his salt ever visited the Carolinas without searching for *Shortia*. Like the lost chord, it was pursued.

Meanwhile, Dr. Gray examined his collection of Japanese plants and was amazed to find a specimen almost identical to the plant in Michaux's herbarium, so he knew he was on the trail.

In 1877 a young boy, G. M. Hyams, picked up a plant on the banks of the Catawba River near the town of Marion in McDowell County, North Carolina. Luckily it had been collected in flower. The boy's father, an amateur herbalist, announced to the botanical world the finding of *Shortia*.

Although Gray did not dispute the find, he did question the site. Michaux had said high mountains, not along the banks of a low-lying river.

So the search went on.

In the autumn of 1886, one Professor Sargent visited the headwaters of the Keowee River, the great eastern fork of the Savannah, in the mountains of North Carolina. At a place called Hog Back – soon renamed Sapphire – he met a colleague, Mr. Frank Boynton. They began to trade and examine plant specimens. One particular plant held their fancy, and a third member of the group, a Mr. Stiles, said, "That's *Shortia* you have in your hand."

Sure enough, the leaf was *Shortia*, found just ninety-eight years after it was first discovered, probably near the same spot. Local newspapers reported the following spring they saw it "growing in great masses, acres, in fact, which were as thickly covered as clover fields. Wagon-loads of it were eventually taken away and still there appeared to be no diminution of its abundance."

A flowering plant was sent to Gray at Harvard but he never had the opportunity of seeing *Shortia* blooming in the wild.

If only our legislators could show such dedication in finding a way to erase the federal deficit. They appear, however, to view money as the autumn leaf fall – never ending.

Oconee-bells is the popular name, the name the local people use, referring to the Oconee area of the Appalachians. And, of course, it's a very popular plant with the wildflower cognoscenti. The shiny evergreen leaves turn to red or bronze in the fall and creep low to the ground. It must have a moist but well-drained spot with very acid soil, in the shade. No lime is allowed – even water that passes over or through an old concrete foundation will prevent the plant from ever doing well. It needs a winter mulch in USDA Zone 5.

No other flower is quite as beautiful in this class of ground cover. The often nodding blossoms are bell-like in form. Their white, waxy petals evidence a soft pink glow and are delicately scalloped at the edges. Add to this the evergreen foliage with its autumn tints of bronzy-red and you know why gardeners love to have it.

IN THE PINEY WOODS

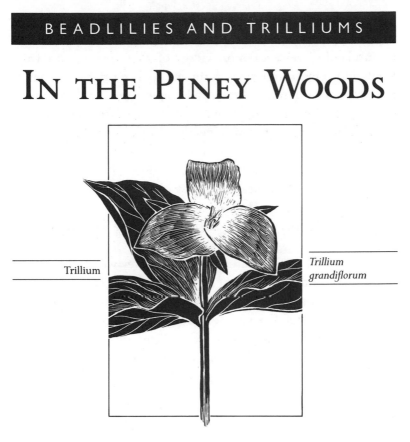

Trillium

Trillium grandiflorum

There are two wild gardens I have known and worked within. One encompasses wildflowers that grow at the wild end of the garden; the other is the surrounding woods that I have known and walked in for years.

Even though it's called a wild garden, the one close to home is always tended. If a weed appears, it's removed. If a tree branch falls, it's carted away. The leaves that fall and cover the flowers are raked into piles and taken to compost. And if a plant vanishes for whatever reason, it's replaced. Not so in the woods, although large branches that fall and block pathways are pulled out of the way.

The woods I write about were fields until the end of the last century. The trees are all second growth, sprouting along both sides of low stone walls that once marked the boundaries of pastureland. Twelve or more acres of that rocky earth were needed to support one small farm family. The original woods of hemlock, pine, beech, hickory, and maple were cut down in the early 1800s in the spirit of expansion. The hemlocks got the final blow when tannin was needed to cure the leather that shod the Civil War.

Over the years of living on this piece of land, we have developed trails. Our meandering pathways have plenty of overhead clearance, since I have always believed that a person should be able to see his or her domain while wearing top hat and tails.

A short way into the area called the piney woods is a bed of beadlilies, *Clintonia borealis*. (The genus is named in honor of De Witt Clinton, statesman and naturalist from New York State; *borealis* means "of the northern regions.") The first plant appeared out of nowhere about eleven years ago, probably from seed dropped by a bird. Two years later there were three plants, and now, beneath a canopy of gray birch trees and young white pines, a colony is flourishing. Here is a wildflower that not only bears pendent yellow flowers but also produces pretty blue berries and a rosette of basal leaves that stay green and shiny all summer.

Indians used both leaf and root of the beadlily to treat burns and rabid dog bites. Scientists today say the root contains an anti-inflammatory and estrogenic diosgenin, which is used to manufacture progesterone, and advise more researchers to investigate its chemical makeup.

About twenty feet away is a small colony of white trilliums, in this case the great trillium *(Trillium grandiflorum)*. These trilliums have been here for twenty years to my knowledge and probably many more. Each spring I make a pledge to watch for seed and plan eventually to raise seedlings for the wild garden. But trilliums take seven years from seed to flower, and somehow other projects always seem to get in the way. Dig them up? Not wise, because the forest floor in our woods consists of layers of rock with little topsoil, and the tuberous roots go very deep. For every plant that survived the shovel, three would die; it's not worth the odds.

Never pick these flowers in the woods. The three leaves just below the flower are the only ones the plant has. Without them the tuber below cannot produce food for the following year, will not flower, and often just dries up and dies. I could move some of them, but I won't. The purpose of the woods is to let everything be, just lending a hand on occasion.

Beyond the trilliums, the path takes a sharp turn to the left and goes down a fairly steep hill. The hill is entirely planted with rows of white pines, an effort at soil conservation begun many years ago. The needles are slippery underfoot, and care is needed, especially in autumn when the year's crop begins to fall.

Along the edge of the pathway, a few scant inches from the tread of heavy boots, are the rattlesnake plantains, *Goodyera repens*. (The genus name honors John Goodyer, a seventeenth-century British botanist who assisted in the production of *Gerard's Herbal*; *repens* means "creeping.") The orchid flowers are small and greenish white, borne on one side of a spike that ranges between five and ten inches high. They are quite beautiful but not the highlight of the plants.

No, it is the leaves that make *Goodyera* so attractive. They shine like small brooches made of copper then inlaid with silver tracings. Usually about one inch long, they grow in tufts from the creeping rhizome beneath and often form small jewellike colonies, poking up through leaves and needles as they grow. In fact, the common name refers not to the American Indians' use of the root to treat snakebite but rather to the similarity of these patterns to those on a snake's underbelly. The Indians also made a tea from *Goodyera* for treating pleurisy. Physicians once prescribed fresh leaves steeped in milk for swollen lymph nodes. But the rattlesnake plantain is now too scarce to be harvested for such uses.

Just a few short strides from the bottom of the hill, nestled in a little plot of ferns and deerberries *(Vaccinium neglectum* – a northern relative of the southern farkleberry), sits our colony of pink moccasin flower, *Cypripedium acaule.* (The genus name is from *Kypris,* an epithet for Venus, and *pedilon,* "slipper"; *acaule* means "stemless," and indeed, the leaves arise directly from the roots.) The fragrant flowers drop from the end of a ten-inch scape and bear an inflated sac. There are two leaves, each about eight inches long.

Bumblebees are the pollinators, and they must use force to push themselves inside the slipper. You can often hear their buzzing as they crawl about looking for nectar. Sometimes a very large bee is trapped and perishes in this pink prison.

Moccasin flowers were once called the American valerian and were widely used in the nineteenth century for nervous headaches and what was, in those days, called hysteria. The orchid tubers were thought to resemble testicles. So according to the doctrine of signatures (a belief that if a flower resembled an animal organ, it could be used to treat that organ's disability), they were used as aphrodisiacs.

The old books say that the moccasin flower was once the most common of all the wild orchids and vast colonies bloomed in every woods. But now the pickers and the developers have done their worst, and no longer do the deep-pink slippers bloom with such abandon in the acid soil where pines and hemlocks grow.

All in all, I enjoy a walk through the woods where, glancing down, I can see these and the other self-sown flowers in the place where they first began. That's better than moving them closer to a civilization that has extinguished so many of their kingdom.

A MAY WILDFLOWER

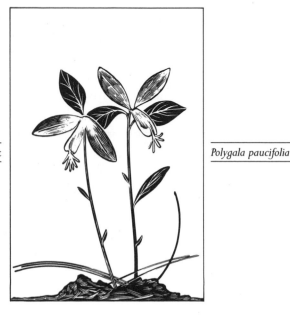

Fringed milkwort | *Polygala paucifolia*

For years I used to walk through a nearby woods on an old logging trail. The ruts left by the loggers had long since filled in with forest litter, enabling ferns and mosses to spread with abandon. Here and there small pools of water—formed by the rock ledges just beneath the soil—were home to spring peepers that would raise their voices to the filtered sun but quickly shut up as I passed by.

A number of wildflowers bloomed along that trail. In early spring the tiny white violets would appear among the mosses and grasses like brilliant stars in a sky of green, soon to share their turf with the larger purple violets and the lengthening crosiers of the common bracken. In early summer the hawkweeds would dot the grasses with yellow, to be followed in August by beechdrops and Indian pipes. For October the leaves above the trail would become an autumn medley, and finally the yellow witch hazel would wind up the forest year.

But my favorite time was the end of May, when the *Polygala paucifolia* would appear. Nicknames include fringed polygala, flowering wintergreen (which it resembles in form), fringed milkwort, gaywings, and bird-on-the-wing, this last because they resemble swarms of tiny winged creatures (though in this case mauve butterflies rather than birds). The genus name combines *poly,* "many," and *gala,* "milk," because people once believed that infusions of this plant would promote milk production. *Paucifoila* means "few leaves."

These are small purple-pink flowers with a prominent fringed crest. Two large petals, flaunted at many angles, are carried above simple, shiny green leaves. The plants are only a few inches tall.

Like violets, fringed polygala is cleistogamous, that is, it bears two sets of flowers. One is aboveboard and usually attractive to insects. The other is usually way down on the stem, but in the case of fringed polygala, it is on a subterranean stem where pale, pouchlike flowers never open and pollinate themselves.

The other wildflower *Polygala* resembles the field milkworts. *P. sanguinea* is an annual plant with numerous but very small pink-to-red flowers that cluster in a cloverlike head on a one-foot stem bearing narrow leaves. A green form is mistakenly called *P. viridescens.* These were the plants generally used to feed cows.

One *Polygala* called Seneca snakeroot *(P. senega)* produces small, pealike flowers on a fourteen-inch stem and grows in rocky woods from New Brunswick south to Georgia then west to Arkansas. The American Indians used the root to make a tea for relieving pneumonia, chronic bronchitis, and asthma, since the treatment was thought to relax respiratory mucous membranes. It was first introduced to England in 1735 by a Scottish physician, Dr. Tennant, who noticed its use as a treatment in rattlesnake bites, hence the name of Seneca snakeroot.

In the woods, fringed polygala is better left alone – that is, unless you find a stand in danger of destruction by developers. Then any effort is worth a try. To begin with, it wants a cool, very acid soil with lots of humus, perfect drainage, and shade for most of the day. Many experts insist on leaving some of the original soil with the roots when transplanting in case essential soil organisms are not present in the plants' new home.

Used as a ground cover, *P. paucifolia* will slowly spread under rhododendrons and other acid-loving shrubs. The plant seems to benefit from the cool of having rocks at its roots and is often found on slopes well scattered with rock formations. If you do find a source for this wildflower, a pine-needle mulch is helpful.

To propagate, use seed as soon as it is ripe. Stem cuttings from new growth in early summer will root in sandy, acid peat in a terrarium but will take a year to get a good root system.

Last week I headed for the trail only to find that it's nothing but a mass of muddy ruts and broken stones. The forest is once again being cut. Instead of the heady smell of wood loam and fresh mountain air, the odor of gasoline mixes with the pungent smell of tannic acid from the shattered oaks. The colony of fringed polygala is gone.

MAIDENHAIRS AND CINNAMON STICKS

Prothallium × 5
(female)

(Male)

Sperm × 16

For years whenever we have gone for a walk in the woods, any woods in the Northeast, I have kept my eye on the ground. Not from fear of stumbling or losing my way, but simply because I don't want to miss a thing, either plant or animal. After all, the views above are merely the same old brown tree branches silhouetted against the same old blue or gray sky.

One of the plants that I'm always looking for is the maidenhair fern. I consider it one of the most beautiful ferns in the forest, but it's not common. When I do spot a clump of these graceful fronds growing at the edge of a woods, I call everyone over with the cry, "I've found the elusive maidenhair!"

Once found, it's duly admired, and occasionally I might take a picture. But we never dig it up, for most large nurseries in the United States usually keep it in stock.

The maidenhair fern is but one of the many beautiful members of this family, which includes some of the oldest plants on the face of the earth. When you look at a typical fern, you are looking at a plant that stretches back some 350 million years to the Paleozoic era, when the carbonized remains of these plants formed the vast coal beds that are mined today.

In spring the new, coiled fronds (called fiddleheads) emerge from the ground. From then until early winter, when the fronds stand out against the virgin snow like pen lines on white paper, ferns are delightful additions to the shady garden.

Ferns number some ten thousand species worldwide, far fewer than the three hundred thousand species of seed-bearing plants. Yet with some one hundred species available for cultivation in a fern bed, they become an interesting plant family for gardeners who wish to specialize. In a reasonably small area, a number of species may be grown. And to approximate the terrain they are found in when growing naturally, the gardener should provide positions for deep shade, light shade, and an open, partially sunny spot.

Soil should be light and moist. Heavy soils can be adapted to fern culture with the addition of leaf mold or peat moss. Their roots are thin and wiry and, except for a few species (the hay-scented fern, *Dennstaedtia punctilobula,* for example, and the common bracken, *Pteridium aquilinum),* resent the thickness of clay soil. Sandy soils must also contain humus to provide the constant moisture that fern roots require—though only a few species can tolerate standing water. If water is needed, the gardener can easily supply it with a hose on a weekly schedule.

Bring in a few rocks to help vary the terrain if your backyard is unnaturally (for ferns) flat. In nature these plants ramble over gentle slopes or sprout from a tiny bit of leaf litter lodged between boulders.

THE FERN LIFE CYCLE

Ferns do not bear flowers and seeds but have a busier life cycle than the flowering plants. They produce spores encased in tiny capsules called *sori.* These sori turn brown as they age. When they mature and the air is dry, their walls bend back, and millions of dustlike spores go into the air. If it's raining, the sori remain closed to protect the spores from clumping together and being destroyed by heavy raindrops. One of the ways of identifying ferns is by comparing the various sori, since they vary from species to species as fingerprints vary among people.

The spore drifts to earth and, with a proper combination of temperature and moisture, grows into a flat, heart-shaped structure called a *prothallium,* which at maturity is about the size of an aspirin tablet. Separate male and female organs grow on the underside of the prothallia, one producing eggs and the other sperm. Using dew, fog, rain, or even melting snow, the sperm swim to an egg and fertilize it. Soon an embryo fern begins to develop.

Although it's an interesting part of natural history, and it certainly works for ferns, mosses, and the like, this life cycle is not very efficient. So Nature took a different approach with the flowering plants, creating the blossom that contains pollen and egg-manufacturing abilities and an enclosed embryo for developing seeds.

PROPAGATING SPORES

If you want to enlarge your collection of ferns for the wild garden, the best and most adventuresome way is to grow your own plants from spores collected around the world.

First, absolutely sterile conditions are mandatory for home

propagation of spores. You don't need a high-tech lab, but fern spores are easily invaded by mold, fungus, and a lot of other undesirables.

Ripe spores can be sown at any time of the year. Use three- or four-inch clay pots, scrubbed and sterile. Clay is necessary to ensure both the free circulation of air and the absorption of water. Place a piece of crockery over the drainage hole of each pot and fill to one inch of the rim with a sterilized mix of one third potting soil, one third peat moss, and one third sharp or builder's sand. Lightly tamp the mix with a knife or spatula, making the surface smooth and level. If you are unsure of the sterility of the mix, put the filled pots into a 250°F oven and bake them for two hours. Make sure everyone else is gone, since this will not smell like baking brownies. And don't use a microwave.

Next soak the pots by sitting them in a shallow basin of water until both clay and soil are completely saturated, then drain off the excess.

Using a piece of folded paper, cast the spores, one species to a pot. Label each pot with the date and species, since baby ferns all look alike. Cover the pots with a sheet of glass or rigid plastic, and put them in a warm spot at 65° to 70°F (18° to 21°C) under dim light. Since our house is old and chilly at times, I keep fern propagation pots on a heating cable below the level of the windows. At all times keep the pots away from the direct rays of the sun. You are trying to duplicate the conditions found on the forest floor, and sunlight will impede germination.

Check the medium for signs of dryness. If drying begins, soak the pots again. Don't water from the top because the germinating spores should never be disturbed. If condensation on the glass becomes too heavy, remove the glass for a while. A thin beading of water is fine, but not huge drops of indoor rain.

Many species germinate within a few days; others take a few

weeks, so be patient. As the prothallia grow, a green cast will appear on the mix surface. In about three months, they will reach their full size. If you get excellent germination, thin the prothallia to about an inch apart. Falling condensation from the glass should provide enough water for the sperm to swim to the eggs, but you might have to mist the soil surface if it appears dry.

The tiny ferns will now begin to develop. When three or more fronds have appeared, transplant the seedlings to individual pots. It takes about two years for a plant to mature.

A Few Wild Ferns

Our fern garden is built against the eastern corner of the north side of the house. We used fieldstones to build a low wall to contain the royal fern. The ground in front of the wall was mostly clay, so after removing the second-rate turf that makes up our lawn, I worked in a bale of partially moistened peat moss and a bushel of leaf litter from the woods.

A nearby gutter provides a great deal of moisture during and after rains. When rains are sparse, I haul out the hose to keep the soil moist.

Light is bright on the fern bed most of the day. But the only sun that falls on the ferns in front of the wall is in late afternoon, and much of that is shaded by the lower branches of a weeping birch.

The centerpiece of the garden is a cultivar of the royal fern (*Osmunda regalis* var. *spectabilis*), *Osmunda* being a form of *Osmunder*, a name for Thor, the Scandinavian deity. Roots of this fern when gathered in Florida have been used as a potting medium for orchids. In their native haunts, royal ferns can reach ten feet in height, but this particular type settles for six feet in the garden. The parent of this cultivar is at home in the northern woods and does need attention to watering; in nature it's often found growing next to streams or directly in bogs. If given adequate moisture it can tolerate some sun, but it does better in light shade. The manner of growth is a crown rather than runners, so the plant spreads slowly. Leaflets turn golden brown in autumn.

Another *Osmunda* is the cinnamon fern *(O. cinnamomea)* noted for its fertile leaves—bright green at first but turning to a rich cinnamon brown and resembling the sticks used to mull cider. The stalks are also dressed with woolly tufts of cinnamon color but bear vigorous sterile leaves without sori; this fern thrives in moist, acid soil. The interrupted fern *(O. claytonia)* has two or more fertile leaves that interrupt the normal leaves on a stem.

Christmas fern *(Polystichum acrostichoides)* is, as its name implies, green for Christmas, and cut fronds make excellent holiday decorations. The genus name refers to the several rows of sori, or *stichoi;* the species name likens this fern to another genus. Plants grow about three feet high. Its sterile leaves remain green throughout the winter while the others wither, although sterile leaflets are often burned with frost. This fern will take some sun if given damp soil, but it likes shade. It transplants well.

Sensitive or bead ferns *(Onoclea sensibilis)* are grown both for their leaves, which are decidedly unfernlike, and their spore-bearing fertile spikes, which look like beaded feathers and were very popular in Victorian times for dried arrangements and shadow-box pictures (along with coils of human and animal hair). The genus is from the Greek *onos,* "vessel," and *kleio,* "to close," referring to the closely rolled fertile fronds.

They are termed sensitive because the leaves die quickly when first touched by frost. But for most of the year they offer a pleasing contrast to the typically ferny look of the others. They do become invasive when conditions are right but have never been a problem in our garden. They will grow in partial sun or shade.

Lady fern *(Athyrium filix-femina)* grows about thirty inches tall and likes a position in moist, partial shade, though it will live – but not well – in full sun up north, never in the South. The name comes from the delicate structure of the leaflets, which are very finely cut. The genus is from *athyro,* "to sport," and refers to the many different shapes found among the sori; *filix* is Latin for "fern."

Asplenium, the spleenwort, is usually evergreen with simple or deeply cut or compound leaves. The botanical name is from *a,* "not," and *splen,* "spleen," since the genus was formerly thought to be a medicine for ailments of the spleen, but when named, such treatments were already out of style. Ebony spleenwort, *A. platyneuron,* is a good choice for a spot in a shady rock garden. Although many of these ferns grow best in the more alkaline soils found near limestone rock, the ebony spleenwort is also at home in acid soil.

Matteuccia pensylvanica, the ostrich fern, reaches heights of three feet and is great for backgrounds. It was named in honor of C. Matteucci (1800–1868), an Italian physicist. Because these ferns take more sun than most, you'll often find them at the edge of a woods, lining an old country road, especially if they have a wet ditch for a rhizome- or root-run. New plants appear by runners.

Another choice for an initial fern garden is the florist's fern *(Dryopteris spinulosa),* known also as the spinulose wood fern. When approaching a grove of these plants in the woods, you see the archetypal fern. For cut flowers, this fern usually supplies the greens in the arrangement. The *dryad* in the genus name is a wood nymph, and it refers to this fern's fairylike qualities. Florist's fern needs light shade and must be well watered to prevent burning of the fronds. Plants grow about thirty inches tall and form crowns. One, Goldie's fern *(D. goldiana),* is found in rich woods and has an elusive quality, though it reaches four feet and produces leaves a foot wide when growing in a happy position.

As for the elusive maidenhair, it is the reason I keep my eyes on the ground when I walk in the woods. The botanical name of this fern of great beauty is *Adiantum pedatum,* from *adiantos,* or "dry," for when it rains, the droplets shy away just like beads of mercury and the fronds remain dry. The fan-shaped, light green leaflets are atop shiny, near-black stalks, and the grace of this plant is evident to all. Fronds grow between twelve and twenty-four inches tall and spread slowly in partial shade. Every so often a dwarf form is offered by nurseries.

All these ferns will tolerate temperatures to $-20°F$ and will thrive in areas of filtered sunlight, the kind of light found near the forest floor.

INSPECTOR MAIGRET'S FAVORITE FOOD

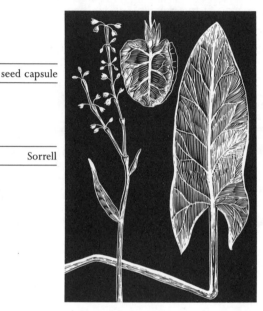

seed capsule

Sorrell

Rumex acetosa

My wife, Jean, is an inveterate reader of Inspector Maigret, that most esteemed of French detectives brought forth from the fertile mind of Georges Simenon. Last week she read a collection of short stories called *Maigret's Pipe,* a volume written to bring back memories of the market, Les Halles, that still occupied the center of Paris when "buses had outside platforms, when neighborhoods were intact, policemen had time for human problems, and car fumes hadn't yet smothered the smell of chestnut blossoms."

In a story called "The Drowned Men's Inn," the inspector and the superintendent stop for a meal at Mère Catherines, a truck drivers' stop just outside of Paris proper. After pondering the menu, Maigret sees that among the umpteen dishes available is fricandeau of veal with *oseille,* or sorrel, one of "my favorite dishes."

My wife turned to me and said, "Didn't one of the members of the Men's Garden Club give you a plant of French sorrel last spring?"

"Yes," I answered. "It's called *Rumex acetosa,* and the plant came from Majella's herb collection."

Jean went to the kitchen and returned with Elizabeth David's book *Summer Cooking.* "Right, here it is: French sorrel . . . recipes for eggplant, fish, lentil soup, omelette, purée of sorrel, sole with sorrel, sorrel soup, and tomato soup with sorrel."

Later that June afternoon, Jean went out to the vegetable garden. The sorrel was full of leaves, both new and old, the plant's diameter being about thirty inches. She gathered a large bunch of the long, arrow-shaped leaves and made two very small dishes of sorrel purée to accompany dinner that night. Needless to say—for I would not be writing about it if the dinner had been a failure—the sorrel was delicious. And I am not an advocate of so-called survival food (cattail hearts and pokeberry shoots come immediately to mind).

Rumex is from the Greek word *rheon,* used by Pliny to describe a plant in this genus. The distinct arrow-shaped leaves immediately identified our plant as being *acetosa* (meaning "acid or sour"), the salad and pot herb.

The taste is tart but good. The lemony flavor is produced by the high content of oxalic acid in sorrel. Never use aluminum cookwear—a problem not faced by the French, since their gourmet cooks would never consider using such utensils. Use only stainless steel or enamel, which will not react with the acids present in the plant juices.

A hardy perennial herb, sorrel has been in cultivation for well over five thousand years and grows wild through much of Europe and North America. The Egyptians used it in combination with other greens, and the Romans ate a salad of lettuce and sorrel in preparation for heavy meals. By the time of Henry VIII, sorrel was used as a spinach and enjoyed by the entire court. The leaves were ground into a mash, mixed with vinegar and sugar, then used as a sauce with cold meat.

The plant can't be misidentified, since only edible sorrel has the large, distinctly arrow-shaped leaves about six inches long on a six-inch stalk. (Sheep sorrel, *R. acetosella,* has thin, small leaves only a few inches long.) The flowers bloom in summer and are small and greenish, followed by a fruit (or achene) easily identified by its three wings. The new leaves that emerge from the crown are used as salad greens or as a vegetable.

Like many root vegetables, sorrel can be kept over winter if you pot up the roots, water them, then leave them in a dark place to sprout. The new shoots are self-blanched and turn agreeable shades of white to pink, making colorful additions to winter salads.

Some discretion should be used with sorrel, since it contains so much oxalic acid and tannin. This is one of those plants best used sparingly. Go easy.

The Maigret recipe calls for washing the sorrel in several waters and picking it over carefully, as you would spinach. Then cook it for ten minutes in a little salted water. Drain it as dry as possible and chop it finely. Put it into a pan with a lump of butter. For a pound of sorrel, add a quarter pint of cream and then two beaten eggs. When the purée thickens, it is ready.

Irma Rombauer, in *The Joy of Cooking,* writes that sorrel leaves may be pounded in a mortar with sugar and vinegar to make a delicious tart sauce, or made into a purée, seasoned with tarragon and mustard for use as a bed for fish.

The *Larousse Gastronomique* suggests a tasty garnish for soups, fish, meat, or egg dishes called *chiffonnade d'oseille*. This elegant embellishment is made by shredding washed sorrel leaves into a fine *julienne*, then simmering them in butter (or margarine) until all the water in the leaves evaporates.

As a special summer treat, gather a handful of sorrel just before breakfast. Wash, then chop them fine. Heat the leaves with butter until they soften, then add eggs for a marvelous omelette.

Jean has an old handwritten receipe for a cold sorrel soup that's perfect for a warm summer's evening. Gather four hand-fuls of washed sorrel leaves. Cut them from either side of the stalks, then chop into small pieces. Simmer them in a pan of boiling water for ten minutes. Add one clove of garlic, crushed with some salt, half a cucumber (peeled and sliced), the juice of one lemon, another dash of salt, and a generous amount of black pepper. Beat two eggs. Remove the pan from the stove and pour a bit of the broth into the beaten eggs, stirring as you go. Return the mixture to the stove and stir over a low heat until it thickens. Add two hard-boiled eggs, finely chopped. Chill the soup in the fridge. Serve cold with some chopped tarragon.

Before the looming of cholesterol on my horizon, I thought we would never have enough sorrel. But now we watch our intake of eggs and cream, so one plant is enough to provide garnishes and flavoring. Once a year now I schedule a sorrel purée; the next recipe will feature a mix of the leaves with bechamel sauce and butter, as a filling for an omelette.

THE HOLY HERB

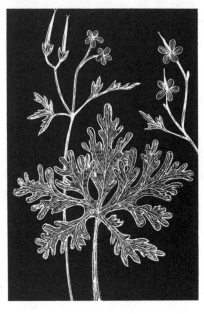

Herb Robert

Geranium robertianum

What most people call geraniums are really pelargoniums, about 280 species of annual or perennial wildflowers and shrubs native mostly to South Africa. They were probably among the earliest plants grown at the Dutch settlement established in 1652 near the Cape of Good Hope, a company town founded to provision the East Indies trading ships. It's quite probable that the ships' surgeons—who were often botanically inclined—brought these plants to Europe.

As early as 1690, one of the three prime parental stocks for what became Martha Washington or Regal pelargoniums *(Pelargonium* x *domesticum)* was known in England ("Martha" or

"Lady Washington" became the popular names for these plants in America, and "regal" referred to their large and colorful blossoms). Ivy-leaved geraniums *(P. peltatum)* were reported to have been brought to England in 1701. And by 1714, *P. zonale* and *P. iniquins,* two of the precursors of our present-day zonal geraniums were introduced to England (zonal refers to the bands of darker green on the leaves). The genus name comes from *pelargos,* "stork," because the seed capsule resembles the beak of a stork.

Early records show that Thomas Jefferson sent geraniums from France to John Bartram of Philadelphia in 1786. Then, early in the nineteenth century, many species were being grown in England and a substantial amount of hybridizing was being done. Between 1810 and 1820, Robert Sweet wrote five volumes on geraniums, and from then until now the popularity of geraniums has continued to increase.

But the largest explosion of geranium popularity came during the Victorian era and continued until World War I, when the cultivation of ornamental plants in greenhouses was banned in order to save fuel for the war. Can you imagine what would happen in this country if greenhouses were shut down to save fuel? Perhaps then more people would appreciate the other geranium, the hardy geranium. The botanical genus is *Geranium,* from the Greek *geranos,* "crane," referring to the resemblance between the beak of the carpel and the bill of the crane.

These are hardy plants suited for the perennial border. Many species have long been popular plants in England, and today most American nursery catalogs list a number of species and cultivars.

But for naturalizing or the wild garden, nothing beats the American native, *Geranium maculatum.* The species name is a reference to the white spots on the older leaves. In late spring loose clusters of pink to lavender-purple, five-petaled flowers sit atop one- to two-foot stalks. The stalks are adorned with finely cut leaves on wiry stems. There is a white form called 'Album', but it's not too common.

To prevent self-fertilization, the wild geraniums shed their pollen before the stigma develops. Thus any pollen has to come from another flower. When weather is cold and wet, the flowers remain male for a number of days before ceasing pollen production and advancing the stigma. But on those glorious days of late spring and early summer when the sun shines in a bright blue sky, the change from male to female can occur in a few hours.

The roots are rich in tannin and are highly astringent, like an old-fashioned styptic pencil. They were also used to treat diarrhea and dysentery. The powdered root is used as a cancer remedy in folk medicine.

Although shade is usually necessary, in the North some sun during the day is readily accepted, and where winters are not too frigid, the basal leaves are nearly evergreen. They grow from a tough rootstock, so plant individuals about one foot apart, and once they're planted, let them be. If a plant must be divided, be sure each piece of root has several eyes. These geraniums are hardy in USDA Zone 4.

Use slightly moist garden soil with added humus. If the soil around the geraniums is mulched to keep them weed-free, they will be encouraged to grow and eventually form a large clump of specimen plants.

Geranium robertianum, native to both Europe and America, is a biennial, but it usually flowers the first year from seed. The common name is herb Robert, red robin, or red shanks, but there are more than a hundred folk names for this plant in England alone, including fellon grass, squinter-pip, stinking Robert, and Granny-thread-the-needle.

Neltje Blanchan, writing in *Nature's Garden,* supposes that the Robert for whom this "holy herb" was named is either St.

Robert, a Benedictine monk, or Robert, Duke of Normandy. But in French, *Robin* is a diminutive of *Robert,* and the name might refer to the robin red-breast, a bird that, according to folklore, if not treated correctly, will cause more bad luck than breaking ten mirrors or crossing paths with a herd of black cats. Until reading up on this threat, I had no idea that if you destroy a robin's nest, lightning will strike your house or your hands will tremble forever. The connection with the bird is the reputed smell, the color red, and the beak on the seed.

About the smell: I am continually amazed at the nasal sensibilities of the Middle Ages. People back then had the ability to live unbothered by an odoriferous world of open sewers, infrequent baths, and problems with drains when there were no drains, yet they complained about a flower's odor. Many authorities both old and new say that herb Robert has a fetid odor when touched. I wouldn't suggest rolling around in a patch, but you will probably never be bothered by any smell.

Anything that has a bad smell is sure to be used in medicine, and herb Robert is no exception. The leaves have long been employed for treating malaria, jaundice, and kidney problems, and as a folk remedy for cancer.

This is a plant of damp, poor, and shady soil, and it will soon spread to the cracks in stone walls. The leaves are palmate, and plants are covered with small pinkish violet blooms from early summer until frost. When the green stems mature, they turn red, and eventually the leaves are stained with crimson. The various rock garden societies occasionally offer a white form, 'Album.'

Never topping ten inches in height, herb Robert is an attractive ground cover and edging plant and, once established, will continue to self-seed. When ripe, the little seed containers go off like little guns, and the seed will fly!

A JUNE WILDFLOWER

Pheasant's eye · Adonis aestivalis

The genus *Adonis* takes its name from a god of Greek mythology. The beloved of both Venus and Persephone, Adonis was a god of great importance in many religions, including the worshipers of Phoenicea and Babylonia, where his name was Tammuz. His mother, Myrrha, was banished for an incestuous relationship with her father, Cinyras, an Assyrian king, and forced to wander the earth alone, until in the midst of giving birth to Adonis, she was changed into a myrrh tree *(Balsamea myrrha)*.

Adonis was too handsome for his own good and many of the Greek hierarchy were jealous in one way or another. (The machinations of the Olympic gods were the stuff of yesterday's legends – and today's most widely read novels.)

One afternoon while hunting, Adonis was confronted by a particularly menacing wild boar, and in the words of Ovid in *The Metamorphoses* (as rendered in English by A. E. Watts),

—A fierce old boar, the dogs had roused him there;
And Cinyras' bold son, before he broke
From cover, speared him with a sidelong stroke.
The beast, in fury, with tiptilted snout,
Dashed from the wound the bloodstained weapon out—

Venus, flying high overhead in a chariot led by a team of flying cygnets, looked down to see the boar sink its tusk into Adonis's thigh and the blood pour onto the ground. After tearing her hair and beating her breast in anger over her loss, she reasoned that if the mother could be turned into a tree, the son could be remembered in much the same way. So she sprinkled the blood with nectar's dew, and one hour later a blossom grew, "born from the blood, itself of sanguine hue." But like Adonis, it is short-lived: Even before the wind can blow the blossoms open and scatter the petals, *Adonis flammeus,* growing wild in the wheat fields of Europe, is cut down by advancing mowers.

Now Adonis was so loved by the women of Greece and the gods were so disheartened by the sorrows of Venus that he was required to spend only a third of the year in Hades; the rest of the time he was free to roam the upper world. So when midsummer arrived, festivals of Adonis sprang up, and the first gardens of Adonis appeared. These were baskets or pots of earth in which quick-growing plants were sown, tended for eight days, allowed to wither, and then flung into the sea—or into local springs or pools—along with figurines of the dead youth.

Pizzetti and Cocker in their fine book, *Flowers, A Guide for Your Garden,* note that when Sicily was a Greek colony, *Adonis flammeus* was the choice for sowing in small terracotta pots.

The legend of Adonis has been used both in fiction and in contemporary horror fiction a number of times. In Thomas Tryon's novel *Harvest Home*—as in its subsequent TV movie, *Dark Secret of Harvest Home,* with Bette Davis and Donald Pleasence—a young man is kept for a year in sybaritic luxury featuring wine, women, and song, only to be sacrificed for the good of the crop. The unintentionally funny movie of Steven King's short story *Children of the Corn* follows much the same plot.

Though I looked for seed of this wildflower in a number of places, I found that only Chiltern of England and Thompson & Morgan listed any Adonis at all, and they had only pheasant's eye, *Adonis aestivalis,* different only in its slightly smaller flower. The deep red buds began to open this week. The flowers sit on top of foot-high stems that sport finely divided leaves like those found on camomile. The plants are truly beautiful, and the color of the flowers glows across the garden.

Since these plants do not transplant well, sow the seeds in drifts directly in the garden in early spring after the soil can be comfortably worked, or start them in individual peat pots. The seeds take about two weeks for germination. They tolerate a bit of shade and resent very hot summers.

I scattered some seeds about the stepping-stones that lead to my sundial. Eventually the blooming plants produced blood-red flowers that popped with color against the gray of the stones— especially after a summer rain. This flower is indeed endowed with the color of blood.

More seed germinated within a clump of bulbous oats grass (*Arrhenatherum elatius* var. *bulbosum* 'Variegatum'), where the fernlike foliage of Adonis was at delightful odds with the soft curves of the blades, and the flowers glowed against the green and white variegations of the grass. The rest of the seed I planted in a few clay pots for the terrace—in memory of the

Greek tradition—where they will bloom for most of the summer, especially if spent blossoms are removed.

There are always marigolds and petunias. But for those who wish for an escape from boring constancy—at least in the garden—try Adonis.

NETTLE, WHERE IS THY STING?

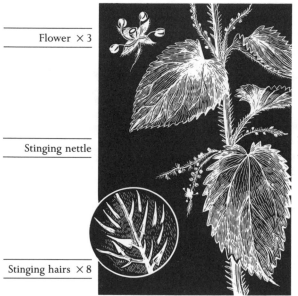

Flower × 3

Stinging nettle

Urtica dioica

Stinging hairs × 8

Back by the old barn foundation that lies behind our formal garden, growing in the midst of a tangle of thimbleberries, is a large clump of stinging nettles. Every year I get stung because I forget just how pernicious these plants can be.

Nettles are perennials, commonly found – as the books say – in waste places (deplorable terminology, since I've often found that most waste places are far nicer to look at than the areas where human development has succeeded), along the edges of unkempt fields and around abandoned farms. The botanical name is *Urtica dioica;* the Latin *uro* means "to burn."

The underside of the leaf is lined with countless stinging hairs, each consisting of a pointed, elongated tube that arises from a plant cell. When the point pierces the skin, it breaks off, and the contents of the cell–which in the case of the nettle is a concentration of formic acid–drains into your skin and burns. Formic acid is the same chemical that ants use when they bite. The contents of one cell can be uncomfortable, so you can imagine how painful a number of these cellular hypodermics can be. (Remember *Them,* that sci-fi epic where the little girl smelled formic acid and screamed her lungs out?)

But one person's poisonous plant can be another person's delight, and the nettle is a case in point.

The plants are said to have reached England by way of Caesar's soldiers. According to legend, the soldiers lacked warm pants and so would rub their legs with the weed, the smarting and burning supposedly keeping them warm.

Karl Brooks, in his excellent book *A Catskill Flora and Economic Botany,* tells the following about nettles:

> Before the introduction of flax, the fibers necessary to the production of sailcloth, sacking, and cordage were made from nettles and many housewives considered this material to be superior to all other linens. In Britain its use was discontinued at the turn of the century because it was so costly to both grow it and collect it . . .

When Germany and Austria ran out of cotton during World War I, these two countries collected tons of nettles for the manufacture of tarpaulins, stockings, and cloth in general.

Chicken and egg producers take note: Dried and finely

chopped nettles have also been added to poultry feed to increase egg production. Older books tell of a greenish yellow dye being extracted from the plants and used to color wool. Finally, most of the chlorophyll used in commerce, including medical ingredients and food coloring, is obtained from nettles.

But nettles are best known as a food, since the stinging properties are lost during cooking. The greens are said to be easy to digest and rich not only in vitamins A and C but in protein and many essential trace minerals as well. The young tops are gathered in spring when they are six to eight inches tall. Later in the season they become so clogged with the formic acid cells that they are gritty.

According to *Eastern/Central Medicinal Plants,* the Germans have been experimenting with the root as a treatment for prostate cancer, and the Russians use the leaves in alcohol to treat inflamations of the gall bladder. Some people keep pots growing on the kitchen windowsill in the belief that an occasional sting will take the ache out of arthritis.

Finally, the leaves, seeds, and roots are listed in the pharmacopeia of Great Britain, Scotland, and the United States as an astringent and a stimulating tonic. Using fresh stinging hairs as an irritant is described as a treatment for torpor, but I think I'll stick with loud noises and black coffee.

JULY REDS

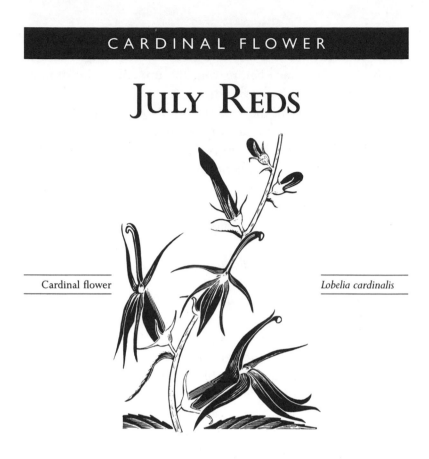

Cardinal flower   *Lobelia cardinalis*

Every summer about the middle of July, when you begin to think it will never be cool again, nothing feels better than a peaceful walk in the woods, especially if you can amble along a creek or stream. Though the air is excessively warm and still, a faint breath of cool seems to drift up from the tumbling waters. Even if you hear a distant rumble in the hills, you know that the rain is still a long way off and you have plenty of time to skip a stone or two across that sheltered pool you've found.

The birds are still. A few gnats bob up and down, and a wasp tests the mud at the stream's edge. The sky is just visible through the leaves of the canopied trees that bend over your head; the only sound is that of the ripples rushing between the rocks. Suddenly you're aware of a flash of color. Bright dots of a rich, deep red dance before you, the uppermost blossom at least three feet from the ground.

No other flower of the woods is as blatant as this. It is that one touch of red found in a Corot painting, the brilliance of a red balloon against the blue, blue sky, or a single traffic light on an empty city street saying stop on a gray and rainy day. Even the bird that shares its name cannot hold a candle to this intense hue.

In the words of Oliver Wendell Holmes,

As if some wounded eagle's breast
  Slow throbbing o'er the plain,
  Had left its airy path impressed
  In drops of scarlet rain.

Seeds of the cardinal flowers were sent back to France after being found "neere the river of Canada, where the French plantation in America is seated" when Rembrandt was a teenager, for they were growing in English gardens before 1639. The popular and species names for *Lobelia cardinalis* describe the shade of red found in the hats worn by the seventy ecclesiastical princes of the Church of Rome.

One of the duties of an explorer was to send home rare and unusual plants, but the name of the European discoverer of this particular flower is lost in time. Linnaeus named the genus *Lobelia* in honor of Matthias de l'Obel, a Flemish botanist who became physician to James I of England.

The cardinal flower has other names: red lobelia, Indian pink, red-birds, and red-flags. But somehow they do not convey the brightness of the most common alias.

It's a lucky thing for the world of beauty that this flower—forever freely picked by those who see it—sets abundant seed and germinates with ease. Otherwise it would have long since passed from the scene.

Even though its home in nature is along stream banks and wet places, the cardinal flower can be adapted to grow in the garden. Most dealers in wildflowers carry either seeds or plants grown in nurseries, because cardinal flowers are one of America's favorites. It would have made a far wiser selection for a national flower than the rose.

Plant breeders have been busy, and new forms have been developed, often with larger flowers and lavender shades and even a white form. A few of them are interesting, but perhaps breeders should leave well enough alone.

Use plenty of peat moss when planting and mulch well to keep the soil cool and moist. Make a slight depression to collect water that falls from either heaven or hose.

Winter kill usually happens when the soil is not moist enough, but mulching well in late fall can help. The best way to have flowers every year, however, is to let a few plants go to seed. New plants will continually arise. Many gardeners separate and replant the clusters of new basal rosettes in the fall after bloom is over, but this can be a tricky proposition at best, especially in the mountain areas where autumn frosts come early.

THE MAN-EATERS

Pitcher plant | *Sarracenia purpurea*

When I was very young and taken with reading comic books, I remember brave men and women flying to distant planets where, upon landing, they were confronted with plants that were richly drawn and heavily detailed, bearing jagged thorns and gaping, bleeding jaws at the ends of tentacular arms. And if Buck Rogers and I parted company for any reason, Tarzan was ready in the wings and would soon be battling the predatory plants of the Congo.

Said Francis E. Lloyd in his classic *The Carnivorous Plants* (1942),

From time to time during the last 50 or 60 years there have appeared in various popular magazines and newspapers accounts giving more or less detailed descriptions of fabulous man-eating trees. The earliest of these, apparently, is one which was written by Dr. Carle Liche and quoted at length by Charles S. Osborn in his book *Madagascar, the Land of the Man-Eating Tree* . . . in Liche's account, a highly imaginative illustration shows that, instead of a native maiden being sacrificed by her tribe by yielding her up to the man-eating tree (possibly a fictitious kind of cycad), a beautiful magazine cover blonde was the lamb brought to the slaughter . . .

Judging by the number of people who show up at our local botanical garden to see the displays of pitcher plants and Venus's-flytraps, the public (and I) want to believe that such things exist—somewhere.

There are more than five hundred species of insectivorous plants found throughout the world, many in North America. They range in size from microscopic fungi that loop themselves around minute insects, quickly strangling them to death, to the impressive hanging pitcher plants of Borneo and New Guinea that ingest not only insects but an occasional mouse as well.

Because these plants have poorly developed root systems and are generally found growing in boggy conditions—high in acidity but low in nitrogen—they have developed the ability to supplement manufactured food with an infrequent treat of fresh meat. Experiments involving the sundew family have proven that this additional dash of organic nitrogen produces more vigorous plants with an increased capacity to flower and bear seed. But insectivores can just as well exist without an insect diet; they simply produce fewer seeds.

So do not give them hunks of meat and do not fertilize them with any plant foods; neither the leaves nor the roots are capable of handling this. My sister-in-law once fed her Venus's-flytrap some kosher salami from a Brooklyn delicatessen one hot July, and the plant promptly expired. Also be careful about water. Never use chlorinated tap water. The plants resent the chemicals and do better without.

These plants are engineered to take care of themselves by choosing insects they can handle. If the prey is too large for the plant, either the plant or the prey withdraws, and the plant tries again with something smaller. If you give them hamburger, the plant begins with food that has long since deceased, and the bacterial decay, already in process, can do great harm.

Along with a passion for water, bog-loving insectivores prefer a high humidity level and, when set out in the garden, do best in a swamp or bog setting. This is easily managed by burying an old bathtub or sink (I once made a great bog garden from an old soapstone laundry tub) or even a plastic washbasin or washtub. If using such basins or tubs, make sure you cover their rims with a few inches of soil. Thus when water is added, it will always level out a few inches below the plant crowns. When growing in nature, the plants never sit directly in a pool of water but are always slightly above the water table. Or you can start your bog with a large, foot-deep hole lined with a plastic pool-liner. Punch a few drainage holes halfway up the plastic – allowing the top of the mix to be damp, not wet – then replace the soil with lots of sphagnum (fresh if possible) or peat moss. A good mix can be made of peat moss and sharp sand; vermiculite can be used, too. Insectivores do not want anything but acid surroundings.

Swamps, contrary to horror films, are quite bright, as most large shade trees have long since died in the waterlogged conditions found there. Except for the purple pitcher plant *(Sarracenia purpurea)*, which can get by with less sun in hot summer, bog residents enjoy and need at least six to eight hours of sunlight a day.

PITCHER PLANTS

The first insectivore to be carefully examined was the *Sarracenia purpurea*, named in honor of Dr. Michel Sarrazin (1659–1734), a Canadian physician and naturalist who in 1700 sent the plant to Joseph Pitton de Tournefort (1656–1708) for cataloging. The discovery was documented in an early sketch by an unknown artist circa 1550. This drawing went from Lisbon to Paris, where it was published in 1601. Thirty years later it was copied and printed in Gerard's *Herbal,* in hopes that someone would rediscover the plant itself. John Tradescant, the great English botanist, found the plant in Virginia and sent a live specimen back to London in 1640. Its bizarre shape and method of obtaining insect food caused quite a sensation in the scientific community.

Nectar-producing glands on the outside of the pitcher send scent signals to an insect passing by. When the insect reaches the plant, it follows a honey trail that leads to the mouth of the pitcher. Then the victim either slips over the edge or proceeds to the additional nectar glands that work in conjunction with glassy hairs pointing to the bottom of this unusual leaf. It's very easy for insects to walk and slide down but impossible for them to walk back up. Eventually, the visitor drowns in the watery fluid in the base and is slowly digested by a number of enzymes.

Just like every family, nature has her freeloaders. A small Canadian mosquito lays its eggs in the pitcher basin, where the larvae hatch and develop, impervious to the plant's secretions. Frequently, a brighter-than-average spider will spin a web around the pitcher mouth and intercept a victim or two from those descending to a watery grave.

Any plant with the cachet of a pitcher plant has a medical history. American Indians used the roots of these *Sarracenia* to treat smallpox, and they used a tea made of dried leaves for fevers and chills. During the nineteenth century, physicians experimented with the plants as a possible smallpox cure, but its efficacy has never been proven.

At least eight species grow in America. *Sarracenia purpurea* has a lopsided pitcher with the lower curve lying on the ground. Leaves come in shades of green and purple and have a pronounced network of veining. The flowers are a deep crimson and bloom from April to August. The plant is found throughout Canada and southward to Georgia and Louisiana in sphagnum and peat bogs.

The trumpet pitcher plant *(Sarracenia flava)* has a narrow trumpetlike leaf with a hood that almost covers the opening. The hood shows veining when young but may develop a yellow cast with age. The flowers are greenish-yellow. Plants are found from Virginia to Florida and west to Alabama.

These are striking plants for the bog garden. Budd Myers, in his northeast Pennsylvania rock garden, sunk a sink for a small bog garden and grows pitcher plants surrounded by tufa rocks with alpines from all over the world. The combination is superb.

COBRA LILY

Discovered in 1841 in a marsh off a small tributary of the Upper Sacramento River, the cobra lily was immediately seen to be so distinctive as to warrant its own genus, dedicated to Dr. William Darlington of West Chester, Pennsylvania. *Darlingtonia californica* is found only in Oregon and northern California in boggy conditions.

The arching dome of the leaf resembles the head of a cobra ready to strike. It's dotted with translucent windows, looking very much like a piece of Tiffany glass. A "beard" just like a turkey's hangs in front of the opening and secretes nectar to draw unwary visitors. The thirty-inch-high pitcher is lined with stiff hairs that point to the well below and these, in combination with honey droplets from additional nectar glands, lead the victim down. The cobra lily is unique in harboring bacteria for the job of producing digestive fluids. It is reliably hardy only in USDA Zone 9, sometimes in Zone 8 with protection.

BUTTERWORTS

Butterworts are small plants having a rosette of leaves that lie flat upon the ground. They are pale green, shiny, and greasy to the touch because of tiny glands that produce drops of organic mucilage over the outer surface. Rolled at the edges, the leaves form natural wells for the digestion of small insects. Upon trapping additional food in the glue, the leaves roll a bit more. It's not an instantaneous reaction, however; it usually takes a day or more. The genus name is *Pinguicula,* from the Latin *pinguis* for "fatty." Darwin was the first scientist to observe the insectivorous habits of this plant.

The most common species of butterwort is *Pinguicula vulgaris,* found in peat bogs and wet meadows in the northern part of North America. The leaves are about four inches long and give rise to beautiful violetlike flowers on six-inch stalks, which bloom in June or July. It's found across Canada and south to Minnesota, Michigan, New York, and Vermont.

In Norway and Denmark the leaves are used to curdle a type of milk called *Taettemaelk,* in which the curds do not separate from the whey; it's also called ropy milk.

SUNDEWS

Sundews vary in size from *Drosera gigantea,* an Australian species with forty-inch stems, to our native species, *D. rotundifolia,* with its diminutive leaves, four tenths of an inch in diameter. The genus is named for the Greek *droseros,* or "dewy," for the glutinous secretions that glisten in the sun like dewdrops.

The leaves are reddish pads covered with tentacles. Glands

on the pads produce a sticky liquid that attracts insects, then holds them fast. After one is stuck, the tentacle begins to wind up like a New Year's party favor and presses the victim into the digestive juices.

Darwin was fascinated by the movements of these usually tiny leaves. He demonstrated the sundew's ability to catch, digest, and absorb insect meals but did not convince everyone that this ability was necessary to the plant's survival.

His son Francis brought plants from the field and divided them into two groups. The first group was covered to prevent any contact with insects; the second group was allowed to feed as usual. His findings showed that those denied insect food did not flower as well and produced fewer seeds. He is also on record as having poisoned some plants by administering acids, and he overfed some with raw beef.

Criticism of his methodology followed. But other scientists grew the plants from seed under more strictly controlled conditions and found Francis Darwin to be correct: Those plants given a dietary supplement of insects were more vigorous and produced more seeds.

There are seven species in the eastern United States, the round-leaved sundew *(Drosera rotundifolia)* being the most common; it is generally found where sphagnum moss grows. Flowers, which bloom in summer, are small and white.

If you want to grow these plants, construct a small bog on top of a wall so that they can be seen at eye level.

VENUS'S-FLYTRAP

In the colonies in the middle of the eighteenth century, William Young, Sr., manufactured a patent medicine that allowed him and his friends to make a good deal of money – and gain influence at the English court, and his son, William Young, Jr., a plant collector, was appointed queen's botanist without ever visiting England. Upon receipt of his first salary, he did go to

London, where he studied some botany, but he soon returned to winter in the Carolinas. There in 1767 he collected a number of plants, including the most sensational ever: the Venus's-flytrap or Tippitiwitchet *(Dionaea muscipula)*. Because of this botanic sensation, Young's reputation was far greater than he ever deserved.

The Venus's-flytrap is the best known of all the insectivores. It conjures up images of giant, vicious jaws shutting on hapless ladies in abbreviated sunsuits foraging the jungles for black orchids.

Found only in bogs of North and South Carolina, the Venus's-flytrap was first discovered by the governor of North Carolina, Arthur Dobbs, in 1759. He published the following description:

> But the great wonder of the vegetable kingdom is a very curious unknown species of sensitive; it is a dwarf plant . . . leaves are like a narrow segment of a sphere, consisting of two parts, like the cap of a spring purse, the concave part outward, each of which falls back with indented edges (like an iron spring fox trap); upon anything touching the leaves, or falling between them, they instantly close like a spring trap . . . it bears a white flower; to this surprising plant I have given the name of Flytrap Sensitive.

Dionaea is one of the Greek names for Aphrodite and Venus is her Roman equivalent; *muscipula* means "fly-catcher." I doubt if the title is misogynist in nature; it was probably named with a touch of irony. There is only one species, and it's hardy only in USDA Zone 8 or warmer.

The traps are green in poor light and turn a deep crimson as the light increases. The surface of each trap has three hairs that respond to touch by closing the trap. The time needed to snap

shut can be several seconds or less than half a second, depending on the age of the traps and the outside temperature (the
greater the heat, the faster the traps close). A trap will usually
reopen within a day if the gardener cheats and touches the
trigger hairs with a broomstraw or other object used to demon-
strate the plant's unusual abilities. If the plant does catch a
meal, it's digested in four to twenty days, depending on the size
of the victim. The signal hairs must be touched twice within
some twenty seconds or they will not close, probably to prove
to the leaf that it has a live catch. After a few meals or with
increasing age, the traps turn black and fall off, and new traps
grow. Mature plants can have many traps at the same time.

If grown in a pot, this plant must have a dormant period
during the winter with temperatures of about 40°F. It will not
do as a houseplant unless the temperature is strictly regulated.
In late spring, the plants send up small white flowers with wavy-
edged petals that are dainty and attractive.

SUMMER AT THE POND

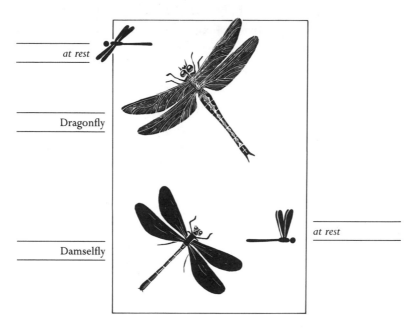

at rest

Dragonfly

Damselfly

at rest

Add water to a garden – in the form of a pond, a small pool, or even a plastic tub sunk into the ground – and certain small visitors will arrive. Frogs inevitably find their way, ready for bathing on a hot day. Small butterflies called skippers will caper along the damp ground at the pool's edge. If the pool is large enough, water birds will fly down looking for the frogs, tadpoles, small fish (either added by the owner or brought from other ponds as eggs clinging to the feet of water-loving birds), and water insects that will proliferate as spring advances into summer.

To me the most interesting visitors are the dragonflies and the damselflies. They are very similar except when resting. Then the dragon holds its wings outstretched like a small airplane, and the damsel folds them neatly over the body.

Fossils of these insects date back some 300 million years, and the originals had wingspans over a foot long. Today they are much smaller. The green heroic darner *(Epiaeschna heros)*, for example, which ranges from Mexico to Quebec, has a wingspan of five and one-eighth inches and is three and five-eighth inches long.

The dragonflies' slender "darning needle" body ends in two gigantic, swiveling eyes that sparkle in the sun and obscure most of the head.

Some years ago Vincent Price played a mad scientist in a movie called *The Fly.* One particular scene showed his fiancée supposedly as seen through the many facets of the crazed fly's eye: There were some fifty identical ladies screaming, one for each facet in the fly's eye. And most people think that's what an insect sees.

No, it's not like that at all. Each facet reports only one section of the view before the eyes. The insect's brain then links the views. A flying dragonfly not only sees a vast diorama but also immediately knows when anything within its domain moves.

The insect's four powerful wings move independently of one another. In fact, dragonflies fly quite differently from other insects. Recent studies have shown that the wings twist on the downstroke to create whirlpools of air over the top surface, providing a lift of ten times the insect's body weight. Helicopters owe their design to these creatures.

Both dragonflies and damselflies mate in flight, and they lay their eggs in water. These eggs hatch into underwater youngsters called *naiads,* Greek for "water nymphs." Nymphlike they are not. Using jaws that grasp amazingly fast, these predators capture tadpoles, all manner of insects, even small fish. The term *water tigers* would be a more fitting appellation.

When the naiad matures, it crawls out of the water onto a handy leaf—usually belonging to a cattail or some other aquatic plant—and, holding tightly with crossed legs, splits its skin down the back, allowing the adult insect to emerge. Soon the wings unfold and dry in the morning sun. Then, some thirty minutes later, the new adult flies off in search of food.

There are about 450 species in North America, but the usual visitors to your pond will probably be the heroic darner, the green darner (especially in the Southwest), the white tail, the Elisa skimmer, the twelve-spot skimmer, the short-stalked damselfly, and the circumpolar bluet (isn't that a marvelous name?).

Every morning from mid-July on, when we walk around the edge of our newly installed pond, we see the empty cases of naiads that have recently escaped the bonds of adolescence. Each case is so perfect that even the individual facets of the compound eyes are visible under a hand lens.

These insects are voracious—and they have sharp jaws. They consume many times their body weight in pests, including mosquitoes. But on sunny afternoons when the air is warm and ripples sparkle on the pond, they dart and skim over the water, hovering first in one place and then another, obviously enjoying the gift of flight and the joy of life.

Melissa Blues and Dusky Winds

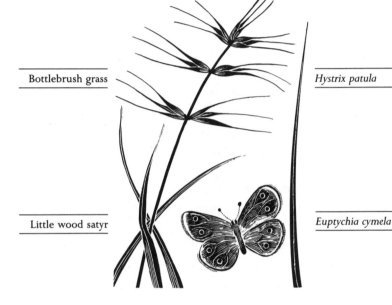

Bottlebrush grass

Hystrix patula

Little wood satyr

Euptychia cymela

I meant to do my work today—
But a brown bird sang in the apple tree,
And a butterfly flitted across the field,
And all the leaves were calling me.

—Richard le Gallienne

And what's a butterfly? At best,
He's but a caterpillar, dressed.

—Frank E. Lutz

Conjure up the thought of a garden in full bloom and I'm sure your imagination will add to your world of blossoms the iridescent wings of butterflies. Flitting from flower to flower, they resemble colorful confetti bobbing in the brilliance of the afternoon sun. For no other insect visitors to the backyard are met with such warm hearts and happy thoughts.

Because butterflies are such paragons of beauty, they are often blessed with romantic and poetic names. A casual glance through the index of Alexander B. Klots's *A Field Guide to the Butterflies* calls forth these, among others:

- The little wood satyr, a charming brown butterfly whose name suggests its rampant flights, seemingly without care, around and through the lush green woods.
- The Melissa blue, one of the blue butterflies beloved by Vladimir Nabokov (a lepidopterist of some note). This butterfly's biggest colony is west of Albany, New York.
- The broken dash, an appellation that refers to a broken black line of scent scales upon the upper wing of this small orange skipper.
- The confused cloudy wing, a Florida skipper with a name that has to do not with erratic behavior but with a case of mistaken identity.
- Propertius's dusky wind, a name bestowed to a pretty Texas butterfly in honor of the Roman poet who wrote love lyrics to his mistress, Cynthia.
- The bog elfin, a small butterfly that lives only in the acid, evergreen, and sphagnum bogs of eastern Canada.
- The Acadian hairstreak, another Canadian resident with a tiny plume upon its hind wing.
- The fatal metalmarks are a family of butterflies with metallic spots upon their wings. But why fatal, one wonders.
- Linda's roadside skipper . . . the reader can make up his own explanation.

But not only are their names romantic; their life-style is, too. What other creature so beautiful begins life as a wiggling, crawling thing? Shakespeare made an unkindly comparison: "The caterpillars of the commonwealth, which I have sworn to weed and pluck away." And then through the miracle of metamorphosis, the larva grows up to forswear all ugliness and becomes instead a winged charmer spending the rest of its life sipping nectar against a background of garden splendor.

Some caterpillars appear in unusual enough costume to pique our interest and give us pause. But they remain caterpillars, and most gardeners would prefer to see the butterfly when its childhood is over.

The butterfly's cycle of life is not a simple thing, and much depends on the complex relationship between the insect and the flower. Caterpillars are voracious eaters, born to chew, and the leaf is their chosen food. Though many species are indiscriminate and will happily eat whatever leaf appears in their path, others can survive only on special diets—in some cases, a single plant species.

The purplish copper caterpillar *(Lycaena helloides)* feeds only on docks *(Rumex* spp.), knotweed *(Polygonum* spp.), and baby's breath *(Galium* spp.). The American painted lady *(Vanessa virginiensis)* enjoys all the everlastings including pussy-toes *(Antennaria* spp.) and the pearly everlastings *(Anaphalis* spp.). The familiar monarch caterpillar *(Danaus plexippus)* prefers the milkweed *(Asclepiadaceae* spp.)—though when pressed, the larva can eat members of the deadly nightshade family *(Solanaceae* spp.). The great spangled fritillary *(Speyeria cybele)* will feed only on violets. Many times this preference for a specific food is so intense that female butterflies lay their eggs either on or nearby a preferred larval food. (Lepidopterists use these clues as aids to identification.)

Once the caterpillar stage is over and the larva has stored enough energy on its diet of leaves, it turns itself into a *pupa,* or *chrysalis*—the more romantic term reserved for butterflies. This is a living mummy case, often intricate in design, covered with spikes, fins, and knobs, and varying in color from a dull brown to a brilliant green with gold or silver dots. At the tip of the spot where the abdomen will be is a spiny projection called the cremaster. Before the pupation begins, the caterpillar spins a small button of silk on a branch, stem, or other protected place and hooks this silk to the cremaster. Sometimes it also weaves a silken belt. Although most butterflies do not dress the entire chrysalis in silk, the skippers, who have features of both butterflies and moths, enclose themselves in a loose, somewhat shabby-looking cocoon.

There, safe in its house, the larva begins one of the most remarkable changes in the natural world, from lowly caterpillar to soaring butterfly. In some species maturation takes only ten days; others require a year or more to complete the process. It is this variation in time that allows the butterflies of the colder parts of the world to hibernate in the fall and safely winter over in their home, to emerge only in the warmth of spring. When the time is ripe, the chrysalis splits and the insect slowly unfolds its wings to straighten and dry.

For drinking the butterfly uses a tongue called a proboscis. The proboscis looks exactly like the largest spring in a predigital watch, the spring beneath the balance wheel that winds and unwinds as the seconds tick away. When extended, the proboscis becomes a straw, and the flower's nectar, a flavored soda ready to be imbibed. The butterfly is a valuable and welcomed player in the game of cross-pollination. When visiting blossom after blossom in search of food, it carries pollen from plant to plant.

If you examine a butterfly wing under a hand lens, you will see that it is a transparent membrane stretched on veins or struts and covered by a myriad of tiny flattened scales, much like shingles on a house. These tiny scales are the powder left upon your finger. The color of the wing is not from a pigment; rather, the individual scales are grooved like the surface of a phonograph record and break up the light that falls upon them into component colors. The pattern of grooves is unique to each species. Iridescence is the result of a thin, transparent film and works like the surface of a soap bubble. Because the color on a wing is the result of structure and not pigment, it never fades. The butterfly wings used in various forms of collage—an artform popular in Victorian times—are as bright today as when they were first created.

The first butterfly to visit our garden in the Catskills arrives on the breath of frost. It's called the spring azure *(Lycaenopsis argiolus)* and is a little over one inch wide when its wings are spread. It often abandons its chrysalis when snow is still upon the ground. Few flowers are blooming when these light blue sprites fly about the hemlocks and pines waiting for the first trailing arbutus or bluets to open. Our scree bed is not far from the edge of the woods, and the spring azures quickly find the yellow flowers of Russian mustard *(Draba lasiocarpa).* Once the garden is in full bloom, they will occasionally visit early in the morning or late in the afternoon but seem to prefer spending the hottest hours of the day away from the glare of the sun and sheltered in the cool shadow of the woods.

The spring azure caterpillar prefers flowering dogwood, which it finds in our neighboring woods; black snakeroot, which grows in our garden next to a Japanese maple tree; sumach, represented by a thicket next to our bulb bed; and meadowsweet, a plant that grows in our adjoining meadow and the wild garden.

Usually at the beginning of May, the cabbage white butterfly *(Pieris rapae)* bounds over the edge of the hill behind our garden and flutters from one end of the border to the other in search of the vegetable garden. This mostly white pest measures one and a half to almost two inches and has a darkened spot at the tip of each forewing. It was introduced into America about 1860 in Quebec and, with the unerring judgment of a world traveler, quickly made a home for itself over the entire continent from southern Canada to northern Mexico. Its caterpillar, as most gardeners know, is partial to all cultivated members of the Cruciferae family. I must confess a begrudging delight in its seemingly aimless meanderings – at least until its more colorful relatives appear toward month's end.

Our next garden visitor is the mourning cloak *(Nymphalis antiopa)*, a three-and-a-quarter-inch beauty with deep purplish brown, velvety wings edged with yellow and a black band with blue spots. Though scientists are unsure whether the mourning cloak overwinters in a chrysalis, it is known to sleep through the snow hidden in a sheltered spot in a wooded hollow or similar place, often leaving its winter sleep while snow is still upon the ground. It then spends most of April deep in the woods waiting for the first violets and visiting the arbutus. The flowers of choice in our garden are the various spring-flowering pulmonarias, which start to bloom in mid-April and continue well into May. A particularly lovely sight is this butterfly flying in and about a bunch of bright yellow tulips. The caterpillars prefer willow, poplar, and sometimes roses.

And at the end of May, when the nights are warmer and many garden plants are in full bloom, the majority of our annual butterfly visitors make their appearance.

The little sulphurs *(Eurema lisa)* are about one and a half inches wide with sulphur yellow wings edged with dark brown to black. They have suffered guilt by association with the cabbage whites, but in the North, their caterpilllars prefer clover to vegetable greens. Peripatetic by nature, little sulphurs have been seen flying far out into the Atlantic, their numbers making a yellow fog on the horizon, often some six hundred miles from shore. Sometimes they land in Bermuda.

When the various pinks bloom in the rock garden and scree

bed, their sweet cinnamon scent calls the tiger swallowtail *(Papilio glaucus)* from the wildflowers of the field into the cultured garden. Its wings are rarely perfect: As the summer approaches you will spot various rips and tears in the edges and often a broken tail. But as long as these butterflies can remain aloft, they fly. They become so involved with the nectar they find that they almost appear drunken in manner. If you approach slowly, taking care not to allow your shadow to fall over their eyes, you can watch that busy tongue at work. The adults, though seemingly so addicted by the offerings of the garden, reportedly respond to tobacco smoke, especially if it comes from the midst of flowers. Often six and a half inches wide, these lovely yellow and black gliders live east of the Rocky Mountains but are represented in the West by their relative the pale swallowtail *(P. eurymedon).*

The caterpillar undergoes metamorphosis within a nest made of one leaf, folded over at the edges, and tied with silk; it is usually found high in a tree, preferably wild cherry or poplar.

The red admirals *(Vanessa atalanta)* appear when the thistles are in bloom. Lovely things with wings banded in bright orange on brown, the forewing mostly black with white spots, these two-inch beauties seem fondest of our garden's yellow knapweed, then move to the field where the burdocks and the pasture thistles bloom. The larva prefers nettles and hops. Near an old barn foundation, where we give the nettles free rein, the caterpillar lives in a silk-lined, leafen home, its edges folded over with silk fastenings, and emerges by day to dine on its food of choice.

When the heat of July begins to build and we start to water the garden, the skippers appear. These insects are a combination of butterfly and moth. They received their common name because their flight is swift and darting. When at rest, their wings are not held high but slightly folded over.

The silver spotted skipper *(Epargyreus clarus)* is the species most likely to visit our garden. About two inches across, the wings are a chocolate brown; irregular yellow-gold and silvery white spots appear when the skipper is at rest. It seems to enjoy feeding on all kinds of flowers. Although many skippers have been observed to be slightly belligerent, they obviously enjoy meeting in tight little groups (a habit of many butterflies). There they will cluster, coiled tongues darting back and forth into the cooling waters, and almost seem to be gossiping, so intense is the mood of these so-called mud puddle clubs.

The caterpillars live in a nest of leaves usually around their preferred food plants: wisteria, honey locust, and other members of the legume families.

In mid-August, when the garden phlox and the four-o'clocks are at their best, one of the few diurnal moths visits the garden. Aptly named the hummingbird moths *(Hemaris thysbe)*, they come on whirring wings, glistening in the light of the noonday sun, darting from flower to flower with great agility. They effortlessly hover while searching for nectar deep within tubular flowers. Their tongues are so long that the maturing pupa has a distinct handle on the side—really a long tube—to give needed room for the developing proboscis.

The larvae feed on snowberries and various species of *Viburnum*. Once they have found a somewhat comfortable pile of leaves, they will form pupae *(chrysalis* is reserved for butterflies) and do a haphazard job of spinning covering cocoons.

Often when the garden is glowing under an August sun and the air is hot and still, a walk in the wild garden at the edge of the woods becomes a delightful thing to do. And while you step along the trail beneath the pines and shagbark hickory, with violet leaves and shady grasses sweeping over your feet, the little wood satyr *(Euptychia cymela)* comes flying by. The color is brown with prominent eyespots on the wings. Only one and a quarter inch wide, this species flutters between the ferns and grasses, sometimes coming out into the open for a sweep of a dewy meadow but soon returning to the woody shade. Satyrs eschew flowers, preferring the pollen of grasses. The caterpillars feed entirely on grass.

When summer is high and the milkweeds bloom in the fields, the last of the monarchs *(Danaus plexippus)* return. Their northward migration was a trip so tailored to the individual preferences of each butterfly that it was probably missed by the gardener. But their return south for overwintering is more noticeable. When the crispness of fall approaches, the monarchs gather, this time forsaking individuality for the spirit of the group.

Monarchs are tied to the milkweed much as bacon is tied to eggs. As they fly north, the year-old butterflies stop along the way to lay eggs in the milkweed plants, then usually die. The caterpillars eat the leaves with abandon, completely immune to the poisonous and acrid sap, yet becoming themselves so repellent in taste that most birds let them alone (though a few stupid ones must taste before they learn). Soon they mature and form their chrysalides, emerging in time to feed on milkweed flowers and then join in the migration back to the South. Sometimes a Monarch chrysalis will overwinter in the North and hatch in the spring.

The viceroy *(Limenitis archippus)* is a butterfly common over the eastern area of the country. Its protective mimicry, which makes it resemble the unpalatable monarch, fools enemies into leaving it alone. Unlike the monarch, the viceroy will be a frequent garden visitor because of its fondness for all sorts of cultivated flowers; it gives milkweed a wide berth.

By now the killing frosts of autumn have arrived. Some of the butterflies of summer have died. Others, like the monarch, have flown to warmer climes. A few have found a safe spot, sheltered from the storm, and millions of caterpillars have turned inward to chrysalides, ready for the coming spring and another season of flowers.

FLOWERS BY TRAIN

Turk's-cap lily

Lilium superbum

Can you imagine the sophistication of riding the Twentieth Century Limited between New York and Chicago, watching America pass before your eyes while looking out clean windows with streamlined corners? Can you see the telegraph poles flash by and the fields spread out beside you in glowing colors against a clear blue sky?

That was the way Americans traveled at one time: There were no overcrowded buses jostling for position with supertrucks on oil-splattered highways that pack cars as close together as wildebeasts migrating across the Serengeti.

Two of my favorite wildflower authors traveled by train: Neltje Blanchan, who wrote *Nature's Garden,* and Mrs. William

Starr Dana, who wrote *How to Know the Wildflowers*. Both have described the trip between New York and Boston, during which passengers could look out on low meadows and marshes in July and August and see clusters of deep yellow, orange, or flame-colored lilies standing above the other plants and grasses.

"Its radiant, nodding blossoms are seen in great profusion as we travel by rail from New York to Boston," wrote Mrs. Dana.

The flowers were the turk's-cap lily and those were the days when it reigned supreme. It outnumbered even the purple loosestrife, *Lythrum salicaria,* itself a flower once spoken of in terms of beauty rather than with curses, before the spread of its blatant magenta spires had gotten out of hand.

The Persian word *laleh* and the Greek *leiron* both mean "lily" and are thought to have first been used to describe the Madonna lily, *Lilium candidum*. That flower of antiquity was once employed as a symbol for the Christian faith but was, in fact, often found flowering in ancient Cretan wall paintings from a much earlier time. *Candidum* is the Latin word for "shining white"; a candid remark is one that is free from bias and lacking colorful nuance.

Turk's-cap lilies belong to the species *superbum*. This in no way is meant to imply that the flower lacks stability or is worthless. Rather, *superbum* is Latin for "exalted," "proud," "splendid."

The one lily of some ninety species that *Webster's New International Dictionary* chooses to illustrate is the turk's-cap lily. This should not surprise anyone who has ever walked the woods and been lucky enough to find this spectacular and beautiful flower in bloom.

It was among the earliest of the so-called exotic lilies introduced into Europe, and it has been grown in continental gardens for over two hundred and fifty years. It was described by Linnaeus and was illustrated by Redouté in his book *Lilies and Related Flowers* (reprinted by Overlook Press in 1982).

William Robinson in his book *The English Flower Garden* called this lily the finest that North America could produce and wrote in glowing terms of its profusion of thickly spotted, orange-red flowers, moved by the slightest of breezes to wave on top of purplish stems that often reached a height of ten feet.

So the press seems to line up in giving support to this magnificent flower.

Plants bear up to thirty blossoms on stems that are usually seven or eight feet high; and many as forty blooms have been counted on one plant. The three petals and their adjoining sepals come in bright oranges, yellows, and reds spotted with black. They are curved outward, or reflexed—suggestive of a Turk's cap, hence the common name. The six stamens end with long anthers coated with dark brown pollen; the single pistil is clearly exposed.

These wild lilies are best placed in the back of the border against a dark background. In fact, nothing could be better than a grove of lilies at the edge of a woods or in front of a rock wall. A perfect place to incorporate the turk's-cap is close to water so that even in the hottest of summers, the bulbs never lack for moisture.

Give the bulbs rich, moist soil partially shaded by low-growing plants, and let the blooming stalks revel in full sun.

Mice have a fondness for lily bulbs, so if you know these creatures are about in your garden, it's a good idea to enclose bulbs in square cages of hardware cloth. Deer like them, too.

THE PESTS OF SUMMER

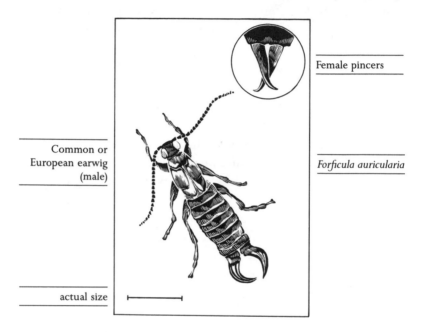

Female pincers

Common or
European earwig
(male)

Forficula auricularia

actual size

Every year I hit the earwig panic button on the glorious Fourth of July. These insects seem to think that Independence Day is the time to scurry forth and make themselves known.

We have a patio umbrella we fold up every night and tuck into a green plastic sleeve to protect the fabric from acid dew. The other day, upon opening it at noon, we were showered with earwigs. They had apparently crawled up the umbrella's post and positioned themselves along the ribs.

Today I opened the side door to the garage, a door that leads out to the garden and when left open frames a view of lovely ornamental grasses and deep blue campanulas. I had no time for the view because the whole inside of the door jamb was jammed with earwigs.

But the final indignity was to fill a watering can and find the swirling water rising alive with earwigs acting like it was the *Titanic* going down. Their little pincers were even clacking out an SOS. Goodness, they are frightful insects, like hornets; you wonder how Nature could have made such an error in judgment.

Earwigs belong to the order Dermaptera, a term that refers to their skinlike or leatherlike front wings. An earlier name, Euplexoptera, referred to the skill with which they fold their hind wings. Entomologists tell us that the pincers, besides being used in defense, help the earwig fold its soft, fan-shaped hind wings underneath the forewings.

They are called earwigs because of the old belief that they crawl into the ears of incautious sleepers and eventually chew their way to the brain. A person so afflicted is called a victim of earwigging. (In the same vein, *earwig* is also a colloquial Old English word that means "to influence or attempt to influence by insinuation," hence, *earwigging* when lobbying efforts are aimed at Washington.)

There are fewer than eleven hundred species worldwide; about twenty live in America. The European earwig (for according to the shape of the pincers, that is the earwig we in the mountains must deal with) was introduced in 1912 and has become a pest in house and garden.

And though somewhat creepy to us, earwigs may have their admirable qualities. Females protect their eggs, rush to collect any that are dispersed, and indeed feed the little earwigs until they are strong enough to fend for themselves.

Ralph Swain in the *Insect Guide* confirms what many gardeners have noticed, that earwigs are usually nocturnal. During the day they search for places to hide—cracks in building foundations, crawl spaces under tree bark—and will take cover in almost any debris (including door jambs and umbrella covers).

A series of glands located on the second and third abdominal segments produce an oily liquid that smells of creosote and are probably used in defense. The terminal forceps can give a strong nip and would seem to be the more effective weapon. Although thought to be scavengers, earwigs occasionally attack smaller insects, snails, and new plant growth, including flower buds and ripe fruit—and I've often found them out at night, eating the pollen produced by various members of the lily family. They have been known to eat mosses, lichens, and even algae.

Earwigs are usually found in greater numbers along the coasts of North America (which makes one wonder just how bad off all those folks are). Like rats and roaches, they disembark cargo ships at ports of entry. Happy to live in garbage dumps and landfills and damp places in homes, earwigs can cause problems merely by being there.

I have an English garden book on carnations *(Carnations and All Dianthus,* by Montague C. Allwood, F.L.S.) that includes a chapter on insect pests. For earwigs, Mr. Allwood points out that chemical means of prevention still lack the punch needed to defeat them. He suggests filling small pots with moss, hay, or crumpled paper. Then turn them over on sticks about nine inches long and place them about the garden. After the earwigs have climbed up the poles and hidden in the pots, he says, shake them out into vessels of boiling water or boiling oil.

Although the punishment seems to fit the crime, I haven't got the hours in the day to retaliate in such a manner. Other gardeners lure earwigs by spreading poisoned bran sweetened with molasses.

Europeans who have lighter hearts often use little concrete cylinders as earwig houses to keep these insects around fruit trees, which they are thought to defend against more harmful insects.

THE GARDEN UNDER SEIGE

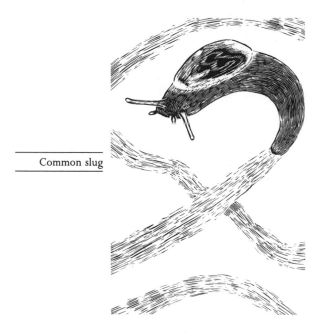

Common slug

SILVER TRAILS

Last evening I walked out into the July night with a flashlight just after a storm had passed and the lightning was an intermittent glow in the western sky. Rain had been heavy, as it usually is during these rainstorms, which the locals call goose- grinders. The wind had knocked down a few white pine branches in the driveway and, unfortunately, broken another branch on my prized Japanese maple.

As I stepped along the grass path at the rear of the yard, I spotted that telltale silver trail of slime meandering along the top of the wall to my left. Sparkling and glitzy like a slim rope of glitter, it signals the presence of the worst marauder of the garden: the slug.

Recent studies in England–where the slug is an even worse pest than here–have revealed the awesome fact that there may be half a million slugs to the acre, a number as difficult to imagine as the national debt or the population of New York City.

More than one species of slug roam about the garden but they are all *gastropods*–a name that means "walking on their stomachs"–and all gardeners know that these stomachs are never filled.

We have in the front yard a peach tree–marketed locally as a Manchurian apricot, but it turned out to be a peach. We rarely have peaches. In the years when the weather allows the flower buds to open, all the bees in our area sleep late. And in the years when the weather ices up, we lose the buds and then any peaches down the line.

This year we have a total of eight peaches developing on the tree. We have been eyeing them every day, hoping to see that Crayola green turn to a credit-card gold. But guess who else has marked these peaches for their own? That's right: slugs! Apparently the brazen beasties see or smell the peaches and climb up the trunk to spend the nights trailing slime over the peach fuzz and hunkering down to eat, eat, eat. And after the peach is full of holes, the earwigs clamber up to set up housekeeping close to the pit.

I've mentioned Montague C. Allwood's book *Carnations and All Dianthus* before. Mr. Allwood has a way with describing pests that put them on the level with mall and second-home developers: too bad to be believed. For slugs (the entry is "The Field or Milky Slug and the Black Slug," a title that reminds one of playing Dungeons and Dragons) the description paints these creatures as being so well-known that only a child of three months would fail to recognize them if they passed by. The slug colors are always described with qualifiers like "off-white" or "milky gray," with lots of greens, yellows, and browns—some even with stripes on their backs.

Now the cure gives me pause, for the author advises gardeners to use quicklime or gaslime dressings as the only effective remedy. With extremely valuable plants, he says, surround their crowns or trunks with soot, an excellent protection, especially when mixed with fine cinder ash, as the slugs are disinclined to travel over such a road. Allwood suggests that powdered naphthalene will kill any slug it touches, and ballast or burnt earth will thwart their efforts to destroy—and enrich the soil at the same time.

One wonders if the next step will be portable lasers? On second thought, going out into the backyard and playing Darth Vader is not such a bad idea.

There are many commercial preparations on the market to kill slugs, but they are all highly dangerous to other forms of life, including the gardener, his children, and his pets.

I've tried the slug traps baited with beer but have never really been convinced that they work. Besides, I like beer too much to waste it on slugs. So I resort to the easiest method: taking a flashlight out into the garden in the dead of night, spotlighting the slug, and sprinkling a few grains of salt on its tender body. The salt kills them without garden damage, but I always feel as though I am reliving scenes from *Night of the Living Dead*. If you are tender-hearted, use alcohol; it's a faster kill.

Just the other day I saw an advertisement in an upscale garden catalog for snail and slug barriers made from three-inch-wide strips of copper that come in lengths up to 100 feet. They can be joined together to make circles for surrounding individual plants and tree trunks, or stapled along edges of cold frames and raised beds. The slug supposedly gets a mild electric shock when its skin comes in contact with copper. It might be worth a try.

In late March the slug eggs are waiting to hatch. Hidden in warm and cozy places like layers of leaf litter or between the curled roots of trees, or safely ensconced beneath piles of rock and comforting earth, the eggs glisten like tiny gray seed pearls, ready to crack asunder and allow their inhabitants to escape into the world and chew.

So what am I to do? Should I go for the poison, watch them whoop it up with beer, or electrocute them?

Now it so happens that as the slugs are getting ready to roll, the roots of dormant plants, including quackgrass, *Agropyron repens,* are beginning to stir in preparation for the warm weather ahead. And the United States Department of Agriculture office at Ithaca, New York, has discovered that a chemical produced by quackgrass as it dies is lethal to slugs.

"The poison is highly specific to slugs," says weed scientist Roger D. Hagin of the department's Agriculture Research Service. "It has been tested with no ill effects on three species of freshwater snails, as well as mammals in general."

Hagin tested the compound for two years in alfalfa and snap bean fields and reports that the snap bean yields nearly doubled because of diminished slug activity.

"We're currently looking at the possibility of using the slug poison compound as a seed treatment in minimum-tillage situations," Hagin says. "We might be able to get the crop plants to take this material up as a defense against slug attacks."

Quackgrass is known to be allelopathic. Like black walnuts, it leaves behind in the soil chemical compounds that stop the growth of other plants. Hagin discovered the slugs' reaction to quackgrass in 1981, after planting no-till corn in a field. He noticed "there were little islands in the field where quackgrass had been growing . . . and in those areas the slugs weren't attacking the corn."

I don't know about you, but I would certainly welcome a way to stop forever those silvery tracks of slime that trail in and out of the garden.

APHIDS

Once aphids have made a beachhead in your garden, they tend to appear with the regularity of bubbles in a lava light.

The only person who could ever have faced this creature head-on is the incredible shrinking man (that hero of an existential sci-fi movie of the 1960s), but the script writers—knowing the limitations of their audience—merely confronted our hero with a cat when he was two feet tall and an average house spider when he had shrunk to an inch; aphids they left out of the cast.

Aphids usually time their arrival to those days in the spring when your crops of seedlings have started to stretch their new leaves to the light above. The female aphid mates in the fall, laying eggs in the shelter of some evergreen leaves on a plant or tree stem or close to the soil where it's warm. When the spring sun moves up in the sky and weather settles, eggs hatch.

The resulting insects, all females, are known by the wonderful term *stem mothers*. These ladies of the stem then produce several generations of offspring asexually; this time they don't bother with the egg business but bear their offspring alive. Some of these children of the stem are born without wings and just stay around in the neighborhood to eat. Those with wings fly to greener pastures. Soon both the stay-at-homes and the fly-by-nights are involved in producing more aphids. And don't underestimate this insect's production capabilities. Ten days after an aphid is born, the virgin daughter is producing more aphids.

Not only do these insects weaken a plant, but their feeding can also distort both leaves and flower petals, and their excrement (which has a high sugar content) can give rise to mildew and also attract ants. How's that for a double threat?

AND FINALLY MITES

Bad as aphids are, at least you can spot them as they sluggishly suck the sap from fresh young leaves and stems. In my gardening world, spider mites are worse: They are such tiny creepers that most of us miss their presence until their numbers and the webs they produce multiply to the point at which the azalea leaves, wrapped in the most delicate of webs, turn brown and shrivel. By this stage it's usually too late to save young plants; older plants suffer a severe setback.

The spider mite, a member of the spider family, spends its life as a tiny speck wandering the undersurface of a leaf. There the female spins loose webs to hold her eggs. Males actually protect unmated females from other male competition by shooting silk in an attempt to tie them down; there is no spirit of parthenogenesis here. Imagine such drama among combatants less than one thirty-second of an inch long.

Once she becomes established, the female lays about one hundred eggs during a two-week cycle. Each of these soon hatches and produces another hundred, all hungry.

The mites are motionless as they, like the aphids, suck the life juices of a plant. But if disturbed, they quickly race about their webbing, looking for a port in the storm. If you place a piece of white paper under the infected leaves and then shake the leaf, the mites will fall and begin rushing about on the paper's surface.

Now I'd much rather fight an aphid infestation because you can – if the invasion is limited – wallow in your rage and crush them by rubbing the infected leaf or stem between your index finger and thumb and generally see the results. Spider mites are more difficult because being so small, you're never sure you've gotten them all. But by the time the gardener sees the problem, it's usually on its way to being out of control so other measures are needed.

The first step is to get out the garden hose. Both soft-bodied aphids and tiny mites suffer from the force of water sent their way with the pressure supplied by the local water company. I do not own a leaf-blower, but it would be interesting to know whether a blast of air would dislodge them as easily.

If the plants are too small to withstand the tsunami, first wash the leaves either with a soap solution—use a good unscented handsoap—or get one of the new insecticidal soaps.

Make sure you read the insecticidal soap label. The leaves of plants like euphorbias, azaleas, delicate ferns, gardenias, bleeding hearts, Japanese maples, fuchsias, impatiens, and many palms will suffer from the use of soap.

With soap in your arsenal there is no need to resort to the many chemical sprays and bombs available in your garden center. The powerful smell of raw chemicals that assaults your nose when you enter the lawn and garden care areas of these stores should be enough to warn you of problems ahead if you breathe or ingest even the smallest amounts of these supposed aids to a perfect garden. The potential health risk to you and yours is not worth the effort. Always beware of any pesticide that gives you a toll-free number to call in case of accident.

But the best way to be sure of knowing that pests and insects are attacking your garden is to walk its pathways every day. Look at your plants with the same care you lavish on your family.

HOP AND HEMP

Hops	*Humulus lupulus*

The hemp family is small, consisting of only two genera, *Cannabis* and *Humulus*. The two are very much alike, yet *Cannabis* is frowned upon by American society, while *Humulus*, used in an important entertainment beverage, is socially acceptable.

Originally from central Asia, *Cannabis sativa* has naturalized in many countries, including the United States. *Cannabis* is the classical Latin name for this plant; *sativa* means cultivated. The common name is hemp, and for generations it's been grown for the exceptionally strong fibers in the stems. Then the fruit, a small achene, yields the drying-aid hempseed oil, in addition to bird feed. Dried flowering and fruiting tops of the female plants are used to produce marijuana, or cannabis; hashish, or charas; bhang; and ganja. Bhang, made in India, is brownish green in color, having little taste but a heavy odor. It is used chiefly for chewing or smoking with or without tobacco or as a drink when infused with water. Ganja, a powerful form of hashish made entirely from the pistillate tops of hemp, is smoked like tobacco. *Marijuana* is a Spanish corruption of Mary-Jane.

Cannabis is *dioecious,* with separate male and female plants. The males die after shedding pollen, but the females live on until killed by frost.

Although the leaves are smoked illegally, there is a legitimate use of marijuana in the treatment of glaucoma. The chemical components of the plant also relieve much of the nausea connected with chemotherapy.

At one time *Cannabis* found its way into every classic ornamental border. In *The English Flower Garden* (1883) William Robinson wrote,

> A well-grown annual of the Nettle Order, *C. sativa* is largely cultivated for its fibre. . . . It is useful where tender sub-tropical plants cannot be easily grown, well-grown plants looking graceful, and are useful at the backs of borders; and a few look well as a separate group. One of the few plants that thrive in small London gardens.

In the 1909 edition of *The American Garden,* by Neltje Blanchan, hemp was listed as *Cannabis sativa* var. *gigantea.* She described it thus:

> A rough-looking plant for bold foliage effects or screen. Best to sow where wanted, but may be started in heat and transplanted. Rich moderately moist soil.

The New Garden Encyclopedia, published by Wm. H. Wise in 1936, notes,

> In this country small patches are sometimes grown, surreptitiously and illegally . . . [and] some are occasionally grown in gardens as ornamental screen or background plants.

But later in 1936 *The Practical Encyclopedia of Gardening,* by Norman Taylor, found no redeeming features:

> It has little or no garden value and the cultivation of female plants is forbidden in many countries because from their dried flowers is derived the narcotic hashish.

The word was out.

Of the two kinds of hops, Japanese hops *(Humulus japonicus)* is an annual vine. It is a valuable ornamental plant, often growing thirty feet in a good year. *Humulus* is from the Latin word *humus,* or "ground," the place these plants will tumble to if they lack support.

Admittedly, Japanese hops can be a rambling terror, wild enough to cover an unwanted trash pile but also able to climb the garage in a single bound.

The leaves are rough to the touch, deeply divided into five to seven lobes, and the stems are *serrate*—a nice word that refers to the sawlike teeth—allowing them to cling to shirtsleeves and garden gloves. The flowers are very small, green, full of pollen, not particularly attractive, and usually hidden by the leaves anyway.

Perennial hops is *Humulus lupulus.* The species is from the Latin *lupus,* or "wolf," because as Pliny said, it strangles others in its climbing embrace as a wolf does a sheep. The English name *hops* is derived from the Anglo-Saxon *hoppan,* "to climb."

Humulus lupulus, a native of Europe, has naturalized in

moist soil, especially along riverbanks and waste places, and ranges west from Nova Scotia to Manitoba, Montana, and California, and south to North Carolina, West Virginia, and Kentucky; it is found in New York and in northern New Jersey. The fruits are used in brewing beer. Yellow glands that secrete the bitter lupulin are found in many parts of the plants but chiefly on the fruit.

A fast grower, this vine has been clocked at thirty feet per season. Plants are dioecious; the greenish yellow male flowers are in panicles on one plant, and the female flowers, which produce the fruits, grow in axillary spikes on a separate plant. There is an attractive yellow form, 'Aureus', with yellow foliage.

The Romans raised hops, using the young shoots as a luxury food. In 1566, Dodoanaeus, a European herbalist called hops a kitchen herb and wrote,

> Before its tender shoots produce leaves, they are
> eaten in salads, and are a good and wholesome treat.

Hops have been used for beer since antiquity. In central Europe, cultivation dates from the middle of the eighth century. They were introduced into England from Flanders in 1524 but were not used in making brew until 1530, during the reign of Henry VIII.

In 1919 hops were still found in London's Covent Garden, tied in small bundles for table use. The shoots were chopped very finely and dressed with butter or cream. Dried hops and leaves were once also used as a pillow stuffing to treat insomnia.

C. Pierpont Johnson, in *The Useful Plants of Great Britain* (a title of masterly understatement), wrote,

> . . . before the use of hops, the beverage always
> went by the name of ale . . . brewed either from malt

alone, or from a mixture of the latter with honey, and flavored, not with hops, but with heath-tops, germander, and various other bitter and aromatic herbs.

Long after hops entered England, brew flavored the old-fashioned way was called ale. The German word *Bier* was used only when hops imparted their characteristic taste.

Julian A. Steyermark in the 1963 *Flora of Missouri* pointed out that in some rural communities, before commercial yeast was available at the general store, hops were employed in baking bread.

But back in the garden, William Robinson spoke of *Humulus lupulus* as a popular and vigorous vining perennial perfectly suited for use in bowers—especially when the gardener is looking for plants that lose their leaves in winter. He also noted that hops will run wild in almost any soil but one slender plant looks great when climbing up an apple tree, especially near a mixed border.

Miss Blanchan's terse entry suggests that the vine's bold, palmate foliage is very effective when in fruit.

Norman Taylor, however, is severe, declaring that the commercial hop is a good subject for agriculture but scarcely fit for the garden. Yet at the herb garden of the Brooklyn Botanic Garden, tall tripods made of bamboo stakes and intertwined with hop vines make an attractive summer display.

Perhaps, as with beer and ale, it's all a matter of taste.

IMPUDENT LAWYERS AND INDIAN PIPES

Indian pipes   *Monotropa uniflora*

Parasites in the animal world are about as popular as Bill Sikes in the fictional. You remember Bill. He was the thief in Dickens's *Oliver Twist* who was brutal and violent, a man who spent his days grousing and eventually killed his mistress Nancy, and whose only redeeming feature was a twisted affection for his dog.

In our antiseptic world of the West, when a parasite is mentioned, most people think of social miscreants or sycophants, perhaps politicians, or every so often a live-in uncle who hangs on for years. If lower life forms are considered, the first to be mentioned is the dog's heartworm. After that it's a blank.

Well, there are both parasites and saprophytes in the vegetable world. But somehow they are neater about it, and when they either cause the eventual death of a host, as some parasites do, or live off the dead, as is the way of saprophytes, the death is so long in coming that many forget the cause.

Mistletoe

Last year about the middle of December we went off to find a Christmas wreath to hang above the fireplace. We finally found the perfect size for an equitable price at a tree stand on the outskirts of town.

The salesman was a tobacco farmer who supplemented his income by gathering evergreen boughs in the woods and having the wife and kids work weekends to twine the boughs in and out of wire frames, then set them off with bright red satin (not polyester) bows tied by his Great Aunt Sarah Clementina.

Next to a pile of wreaths that sat like five car tires coated with green thorns was a large oak branch festooned with mistletoe from one end to the other.

"That's mistletoe," I said.

"Right you are," he answered and looked at me as though I might have trouble reading a watch.

"Well," I said, "I'm just surprised to find it here. How did you get it?"

"Shot it."

"Shot it?"

"Right you are," he said and made a gesture to the sky. "I just get my shotgun and go out in the woods, find an oak branch that has a lot of it and shoot it down. Never miss much, either."

Well, shooting mistletoe out of a tree really isn't any more unusual than the name itself. *Mistletoe*—think about it. Does it refer to mists? Is the foot involved? And does the name have anything to do with its being a parasite? Even though the leaves contain chlorophyll and can generate their own food, mistletoe can live only on trees.

There's an Old World mistletoe *(Viscum album)* and one from the New World *(Phoradendron serotinum),* both belonging to the Loranthaceae family. Here's a case where the English common name traveled to America along with the settlers, who, when they looked up into the oaks and saw a plant close to the one they knew, gave little thought to the niceties of botany. *Viscum,* the Latin name for the plant, was used by Virgil, and *album* refers to its white berry; *Phoradendron* is Greek for "thief tree," and *flavescens* is Latin for "yellowish," referring to the thick, yellow-green leaves.

Since both the English and the American plant appeared to live without earthbound roots—especially on apple trees and occasionally on the revered and mighty oak—there had to be magic involved. Add to this its evergreen leaves, its white berries (which in their arrangement are said to resemble the male parts), its use among American Indians for curing hypertension, preventing pregnancy (as an oral contraceptive), and treating epilepsy (even though modern authorities consider it to be poisonous), and you can see why mistletoe had such cachet. There was even a belief that when used as a divining rod, mistletoe would locate buried treasure.

Back in the days of the ancient Druids, people believed that mistletoe was propagated by bird droppings. Since the old Anglo-Saxon name for dung was *mist* or *mistle* and *tan* the word for twig, the common name became *mistletan.* Botanists now know that the ancients were correct: Birds eat the berries, which then sprout in the droppings left on oak or apple branches.

The practice of kissing under the mistletoe hearkens back

to the Middle Ages and before; such a kiss was supposed to help the couple conceive.

BASTARD TOADFLAX

Another wild parasite is the bastard toadflax. *Comandra umbellata* grows from a wandering rhizome that is parasitic on the roots of various other plants. This member of the sandalwood family also has chlorophyll, so when times are bad with the host, it can manufacture its own food. But generally it would rather find a home in the midst of other plants as a seedling. If you are in the woods and hungry yourself, the nutlets are reputed to be sweet and tasty. *Comandra* is from the Greek *kome*, for "hair," and *andros*, for "male." It refers not to a hirsute gentleman but instead to hairy lobes at the base of the anthers.

The common name of bastard means the plant resembles the true flax *(Linum usitatissimum)* but is not even close as far as family is concerned. Toadflax *(Linaria vulgaris)*, known in America as butter-and-eggs, was a weed in flax fields and looked somewhat like flax until the snapdragonlike flowers bloomed; *linaria* means "like flax." In German the plant is *Krötenflacks*, *Kröte* being a frog, referring to the gaping mouth of the flower. A regional name for bastard toadflax in America is impudent lawyer, and if you think about the look of the blossoms, this might be the best name yet.

THE INDIAN PIPE

Last week during a walk in the woods I spied a very large clump of Indian pipes *(Monotropa uniflora)* growing underneath the branches of a gray birch. The other common names (ice-plant, ghost-flower, and corpse-plant) point to its reputation in the world of wildflowers. I was struck by the strange beauty of this plant: its soft white pallor that seems to shine against the litter of leaves from which it emerges. Although the blossoms usually nod toward the ground, they raise their heads when the waxy petals are ready to open. This particular specimen had changed its floral pitch and was ready to expel a burst of tiny seed. The name is from the Greek *monos,* "one," and *tropos,* "turn," referring to the nodding flowers.

Neltje Blanchan in *Nature's Garden,* gives the following description:

> Colorless in every part, waxy, cold, and clammy, Indian pipes rise like a company of wraiths in the dim forest that suits them well. Ghoulish parasites, uncanny saprophytes, for their matted roots prey either on the juices of living plants or on the decaying matter of dead ones, how weirdly beautiful and decorative they are!

Blanchan was a master of colorful prose, and her descriptions are certainly apt. But somehow in the generation that has produced *Night of the Living Dead* and a spate of horror films, including junkets with Stephen King plus *Elm Street* and *Halloween,* the plant does not seem as funereal to us as it did to her.

The juice of the living on which it feeds is not blood but the sap of a lowly fungus. For the two- to twelve-inch pipes do not themselves live on dead or dying matter but, like many orchids, depend on another agent for survival. Their true root system is but a few short, white cords that lie in close arrangement with a fungus that in turn spreads its threadlike but false roots, or mycelia, in all directions through the leaf mold.

Mycelium is a network of tiny, white branching filaments— much like a piece of cheesecloth—which search for and digest bits of organic matter and humus. Then the roots of *Monotropa* steal these predigested foods.

Hortus Third lists *Monotropa* as a perennial. Because of its method of survival, I thought it would be an annual, entirely at the mercy of finding a store of food. But apparently once a plant finds a fungus to live with, a long partnership ensues. Although it's possible to transplant Indian pipe if a good deal of surrounding earth and leaf litter is moved with the plant, the easiest thing to do for the wild garden is cast seeds in a specially prepared plot where there is plenty of deep black earth loaded with organic matter.

Find a spot in your wild garden where the leaf mold is thick or fungi like coral root abound, and scatter the seeds about. A colony of Indian pipes admittedly would look like a congregation of lost souls—but probably souls of the highest order.

Like many other flowers in the eastern woods, close relatives of Indian pipe are found growing in Japan. The American version was used by the Indians as a healing herb. They used the plant juice like modern-day Mureen, as a tea for aches and pains and for relieving bunions and warts. Watery extracts are bactericidal. But experts warn that the plant's toxic properties are not fully understood.

PINESAPS

Pinesaps are another member of the *Monotropa*, species *hypopithys,* a name that means "under fir trees" and refers to their strict habit of living in the shade of conifers, especially pines, and existing on the sap of roots close to the surface.

The stems measure six to fourteen inches. The fragrant blossoms have short hairs that turn up from the style to protect the stigma from contact with any pollinators other than bees. The plants do not have the ghostly charm of Indian pipes, since their color is a light beige, rarely yellow or red. Unfortunately, like Basil Hallward's portrait of Dorian Gray in the Hollywood production, once old they begin to look like an Ivan Albright painting and are best passed over.

Another plant, called sweet pinesap, bears several fragrant and rosy flowers having the odor of violets. Its botanical name is

Monotropis odorata. Plants boom in sandy woods from Maryland to Kentucky and south to Georgia and Alabama, but I've never seen it.

PINEDROPS

Pinedrops is a one-species genus. Its botanical name, *Pterospora,* is from the Greek and means "winged seeds." The plant is usually found underneath coniferous trees in dry soil and is parasitic on soil fungi. The purple-brown stems and dozens of pretty little flowers bloom up and down a stem that often reaches a height of thirty inches. Here again is a plant often read about but rarely seen.

BEECHDROPS

These flowers are not the only ones of their kind to grow in our mountain woods. Beechdrops, or *Epifagus virginianum* (the genus name means "upon beech"), resemble bunches of thin, pale brown, waxy stems marked with purple lines that turn a rather disagreeable brownish purple as they push up from the ground. They have a somewhat unpleasant odor.

Two kinds of flowers appear on beechdrops. At stem top, tiny tubular blossoms never nod but stand straight up as if waiting for a ghostly bee to wander by. Those farther down the stem never open but still manage to develop seed. Neltje Blanchan writes, again in a wonder of understatement,

> . . . to save the species from still deeper degeneracy through perpetual self-fertilization, [the] small purplish-striped flowers above [develop] mature stigmas and anthers on different days, and invite insects to help them produce a few cross-fertilized seeds.

A tea made from the whole fresh plant is very astringent and was once used to treat diarrhea and cold sores.

DODDER

Dodder is a strange sight. This leafless annual spreads its bright yellow-orange stems throughout the branches of a host plant like vegetable spaghetti tossed by an angry child. Another common name is devil's thread, so called because folks believed the devil spun dodder at night to destroy clover, one of God's plants. The common name comes from the German for "yolk of an egg," referring to the bright yellow-orange color.

The genus is *Cuscuta,* a name of uncertain derivation, and the fifteen or so species in America have minor differences so particular that only the most patient observer will ever tell them apart. And frankly, once familiar with their habits, do you need to know all the individuals?

The seedlings appear normal, the bright color masking any absence of chlorophyll. But soon, like an Indian strangler, this thuggee member of the morning glory family finds a stem and starts to climb, producing slim but penetrating rootlets, called haustoria, that burrow their way into the host's vessels and soak up needed nutrients. These suckers stick with such strength that the stem will break rather than give up its hold.

Only the cells on the outside of the stems will grow longer; the inner cells stay the same size. As a result they soon spiral around the host stem, reinforcing the hold of the haustoria. The dull white flowers are five-parted and bell-shaped.

The Chinese used the seeds to treat urinary tract infections, and the Cherokee Indians applied crushed stems as a poultice for bruises. Medical authorities today generally advise against eating dodder.

SPOTTED CORALROOT

Most people view orchids as exotic blossoms and would not be too surprised if informed that one is parasitic. Such a plant is the spotted coralroot, or *Corallorhiza maculata,* a literal translation of the common name into Greek.

The flowers are small, pale yellow and off-white, the lower lip spotted with purplish lines serving as a landing strip for insect pollinators.

The roots resemble a coral carving made by a jeweler from ancient China, the threads intertwined to such an extent that it's impossible to sort them out. They absorb nutrients from something already in a state of advanced decay buried in the ground. If they fed on bodies rather than plants, they would be true ghouls.

It's under a hand lens that these flowers reveal their true orchid status. If they were the size of marigolds or petunias, people would fight to have them in the garden.

The roots were used as a folk remedy to treat colds and induce profuse sweating.

SQUAWROOT

In June, the squawroot is easily spotted. Its thick yellow-brown stems curve out of the soil and are covered with ranks of tubelike, creamy white to light yellow flowers. The scales—all that is left of what were once leaves—are soft at first but soon become hard and dry, so the whole branch resembles a long narrow pinecone. The genus *Conopholis* means "scaly cones." The plant is parasitic on the roots of oak or hemlock.

None of these parasitic plants have a location in the proper garden; it would be like inviting a rock band leader to a lecture on Spinoza. But in the wild garden of nature they all have a place, and at the domestic end of that wild garden, a few would be unexpected but attractive guests.

THE EIGHT-LEGGED ENGINEERS

Jumping spider
head-on

They have the distinction of being among the most frightful of all creatures, and yet they are a fascinating and unique group, with a scientific classification all their own. Spiders are arachnids. All have eight legs and are wingless, as opposed to insects with their six legs and one or two pairs of wings. Spiders have no true jaws and cannot chew. They must take their food by sucking the blood of their victims rather than masticating them as the insects do. Spider eyes are simple; that is, each eye is covered by one cornea—as in man—and not faceted like the insect eye. Nearly all spiders have eight simple eyes.

And, of course, spiders have silk organs. Insects do, too, but spiders have the most complex forms known. With these organs they spin egg sacs, draglines, temporary homes, strong webs for scaffolding, and sticky webs for holding prey. They can build irregular nets, sheet webs, funnel webs, and orb webs.

They are generally timid, content to follow the spider path. And regardless of Robert Lowell's lines,

> We are like a lot of wild
> spiders crying together,
> but without tears,

spiders are a solitary lot, forgoing any sense of community associations once they pass the spiderling stage.

BALLOONING

On one of those golden days in late spring or fall, a day when skies are crisp and blue and morning dew still sparkles on the fields, newly hatched spiderlings take wing on fresh breezes to see the world. Although it's said to be just instinct, the spider's search for new territory appears as thrilling as any journey with an unknown destination.

Leaving the protective shell of the family cocoon, which is packed with hundreds of still-opening eggs, the almost weightless hatchlings walk upward toward the sun, climbing branches and blades of grass or flower stems and garden fences, always toward the light. Then, at the summit, they point their abdomens toward the sky in what could be termed a foolish posture. Shooting out a filmy gossamer line, the spiderling becomes a balloon, and is caught on rising currents of air and taken to new horizons. As a nature writer once said, all the spider needs is a banner, *Excelsior!*

The journey may be short or long. Some spiders sail far out to sea before their tiny rope is caught in the rigging of a ship. Others, once aloft, fly over mountains and across plains, and a few, like boomerangs, return to where the ride began after minutes in the air. Most never soar higher than three hundred feet, but a hardy few may reach an altitude of two miles, holding fast to their shining thread, waiting to land in a new field or garden.

Occasionally an older spider, still not too large or fat, can be accidentally caught in a rising wind and blown away from the home web. Others, seemingly tired of familiar fields, back into the wind and sail away.

Constructing a Web

After finding a new home, the spider begins its web by constructing a horizontal bridge. I've chosen a female for the example, but males spin webs, too.

Climbing up a branch, the spider stops, aims for a second branch, and shoots a line out into space. She waits for it to take hold, and when it's fast at the far end, she pulls the line taut, and the first bridge is formed.

Now she walks to a lower point on the left branch and attaches a new line. Holding the new line carefully in two of her legs to prevent it from tangling on the bark, she spins and winds as she moves back to the bridge and then across and down the right side, where she again reels in the slack and completes a second bridge roughly parallel to the first.

Next, left and right sides are added, forming a rough trapezoid.

She walks back to the center of the top bridge, jumps down to the lower bridge, trailing silk behind her, like a bob on a plumb line. Once the new line is secure, she walks halfway back along that vertical and, choosing a spot close to the center, marks the hub of the web.

Now it's time to form the radii that stretch to the outside frame. Working first one side, then the other, always keeping the lines in balance, she lays some twenty of them by dragging silk from the hub to the frame, walking over the existing lines, neater than a student sectioning a circle in geometry class (though an occasional spider, for no obvious reason, may do a careless job). When all the radii are finished, she moves back to the center and spins extra webbing to thicken and strengthen the hub.

Walking counterclockwise, she lays a wide spiral of silk across the center of the web, a scaffold to hold the foundation lines in position as she completes the spinning.

So far the lines have all been dry, not sticky, but now, starting at the outside of the frame, she lays a new line speckled with glue. Each turn takes her closer to the hub. When she reaches the scaffold, she deftly removes it, putting a sticky line in its place.

The parlor is now complete.

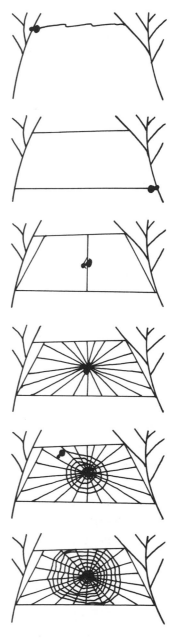

THE ORB WEAVERS

When spiders are mentioned, most people think of the aerial web spinners, those builders that use spider silk. In exchange for speed, sharp eyesight, and unusual strength, they have the instinctive gift of making gossamer webs of amazing durability—webs to trap and ensnare living food. Instead of wandering about in search of prey, these creatures sit quietly in the web center or concealed in nearby brush and wait for the food to come to them.

There are many kinds of web spinners: Some make horizontal webs that infest corners of the house, gathering dust in addition to insects; others, like the infamous black widow, *Latrodectus hasselti,* have earned such a place in spider folklore that thought is never given to their mazelike web but only to their power to kill. Contrary to popular belief, the black widow does not always eat her mate, and there are very few recorded cases in which her bite was fatal to man.

Some webbers are drab, colorless, and small, preferring to spin their webs in dark cellars. Others—large and brilliantly colored—sit with aplomb directly in the center of the web and dare all to come near.

An example of the latter is the common garden spider, *Argiope aurantia.* With a body of velvety black usually an inch in length and marked with bright orange or yellow spots, it occupies the center of a web two feet in diameter that is strung between plants or shrubs in the garden or tall grasses in the meadow.

The *Argiope* female is so fond of her web (or so appreciative of the work that building requires) that she adds zigzags of a heavy white silk, called stabilimenta, across the middle to warn small birds and large butterflies to steer clear. Such arachnid warnings seem to work, as these creatures have been seen swerving and flying over or around the garden spider's web.

When I was young, I believed that garden spiders were among the most fearsome creatures in the world. But I learned over the years that their eight eyes are so weak, they cannot comprehend me, and their only interests lie in food and mating. Their bite is usually less toxic than that of a wasp, and these spiders, at least in most of North America, must be pushed before their bite even begins to break the skin.

If the web is damaged, the *Argiope* female prefers to build anew, though she will conduct minor repairs if the damage is not too extensive. It takes only about an hour to replace the whole affair, and construction generally starts at twilight so that all is ready for the next morning.

You can tease *Argiope* by tapping a leaf at the outer edge of the web; she quickly runs to the right spot, guided by an unerring instinct for tracing vibrations that signal a meal. Do it too many times, though, and she will just sit still, in an apparent sulk.

When an insect (*Argiope* is especially fond of grasshoppers) does become entangled, she responds to the feel of the victim's struggle. If it's small, she quickly kills it. If it's large, more discretion is called for. While a few legs hold the prey, the others wind the panicked victim's body in a tomb of silk. When it is immobile, she bites it and injects a massive dose of poison. She then begins dinner at once or waits, depending on her appetite.

The male of this genus is smaller than the female and starts life in the spring by building a smaller and much less accomplished web. Soon he gives it up and moves to a place at the outer edge of a female's web, living on leftovers and waiting to mate in the fall.

As the days grow shorter and the nights become colder, *Argiope* produces a great number of eggs. She carefully wraps them in a bundle of silk, which is then suspended within the framework of a bush, plant, or shrub and tied with so many loops of thread that the roughest of winter winds will not tear it loose. Then, with the first killing frost, the adult spider dies.

THE CRABBY ARACHNIDS

Crab spiders are exactly what their name implies; not only does their disposition seem testy at best, but they also move back and forth, side to side, with the movement characteristic of their larger crustacean relatives. Like crabs, these spiders do not trap food but instead lie in wait, their flattened bodies easily fitting into an ambush, usually where flower petals join or leaves clasp the stem. They are so patient that you can cut flowers for a bouquet, gather the blooms in a basket, trim the stems in the kitchen sink, put the flowers in a vase for an honored spot at the dinner table, and only then see a crab spider, wondering where the garden has gone, hanging by her dragline right over Uncle Fred's cup of consommé.

Misumena calycina (or sometimes *vatia*) is the common crab spider of North American gardens. Its aggressive nature, coupled with a very strong venom, gives it the ability to attack insects far larger than itself. I was once amazed to see a thirsty wasp, lingering over a drop of water that lay near the attachment of a daisy petal, suddenly confronted by a much smaller crab spider; after a brief scuffle, the spider won.

Although crab spiders do not have the fine vision of jumpers and wolf spiders, studies suggest that they are able to see colors. A. S. Pearse, the American ecologist, noted that 84 percent of the yellow species were seen on yellow flowers.

Misumena has the ability to change color from white to yellow on a yellow flower. The change takes about a week; reversing from yellow to white usually takes five or six days.

Despite the crab spiders' somewhat aggressive nature – notable even for spiders – the female is especially well known for her slavish adoration of her egg cocoon. She will guard it with her life, day after day, until she hears the first rustlings of the eggs beginning to hatch. Then she cuts a hole in the silk, allowing the young to escape, and promptly dies.

THE JUMPING SPIDERS

It's a warm afternoon in the garden. Since one o'clock, the edging around the wild garden has been trimmed, piles of pruned branches and twigs have been removed to the compost heap, and the brow has begun to redden a bit from both the welcome sun and the exertion. It is time to sit back in the lawn chair and plan the rest of what promises to be a fine summer day.

Flies swarm around the white clapboards of the house. A few bees drift about the top edge of the rock garden, looking into every bloom. The ever-present wasps circle about the gutter and the eaves. But there is a closer movement just above your left ear: a small black dot at the chiseled edge of the top of the chair. It stops, then moves again. Not a fly or a bug or a beetle; it is too small and too direct in its movements, and it seems to watch every one of yours.

You slowly turn your head and see a white-and-black striped spider looking directly at you with a deliberate stare. It's scarcely an eighth of an inch long. The collar of your shirt shifts as you nervously jerk your neck, and two large and beady eyes follow; move your shoulders a few inches back, and the spider darts a few inches closer.

You're being hunted by one of the most developed and most amusing members of the spider family, the Salticidae, or jumping spiders. No patient and slowly creeping arachnid here, no curling up in a web to wait for dinner. This spider is the leader of the pack.

Salticus scenicus, the zebra spider, is the most common jumping spider in North America and the British Isles. *Salticus* is from the Latin for "leap," and *scenicus,* from the Greek for "tent," refers to the spider's home. The family is one of the arachnid world's largest, with species numbering in the thousands, and members have been found in all parts of the earth except the polar regions.

Salticus has traded life in the web for the keenest eyesight in the spider world. Its eight eyes are set in three rows. The four in the front row are large – especially the center pair – but the rest are tiny drops of jet, just like the stones in your grandmother's brooch. But make no mistake: Those eyes can see at least a foot with perfect clarity, and the shifting images formed by the eight working together give the spider a perception that reaches a far greater distance.

Jumping spiders live to hunt and are therefore curious about every movement that they see. Able to leap long distances in a single bound, they are the Supermen and Superwomen of their world. And wherever they go, they lay a dragline behind them. If they happen to miss a jump from leaf to branch, the dragline saves them, and they climb back up to begin again.

If patient with your movements, you can coax one to sit upon a fingertip and get close enough to see those sparkling black eyes. But get too close and it will jump.

John Crompton, in his book *The Life of the Spider,* wonders why there are trained fleas but not trained jumping spiders. Naturalists have been able to train *Salticus* to jump onto waiting fingers for food, then to jump ever-greater distances from hand to hand until a leap of eight inches was achieved. "So," says Crompton, "the thing could be done."

Ah, but should it? The idea that *Salticus* could entertain the masses by jumping through miniature Hula Hoops belongs to the days of Victorian peep shows and old traveling circuses. A spider video arcade wouldn't entice the mall walkers of today.

In addition to their agility in jumping, another gift from nature allows these spiders to climb sheer rock and polished glass. All other spiders are unable to hold tight to smooth surfaces, but jumpers have tiny pads of adhesive hairs on the tips of their feet, enabling them to go where they will. Other kinds of spiders may slip into a basin or tub and be unable to climb back out–but never *Salticus*.

Nights are spent in tiny silken sleeping bags sheltered by leaves, by stones, or in the corner of a house or greenhouse. Larger spiders may find their way into your house and garden, but none are friendlier than *Salticus*. And considering the insect pests that they consume, they are more than worth their weight in whatever passes for top currency today.

THE WOLF SPIDERS

Just out of the corner of the eye, one sees a sudden movement as a small, sleek spider scampers up the chimney, silhouetted against the rough, white-painted concrete blocks. It's a handsome spider with a body about half an inch long, covered with a well-groomed coat of black, gray, and brown fur. The spider stops midway up the chimney for just a moment, as though checking to see whether its internal compass is in order. It darts left or right and then quickly back to the safety of the woodpile.

Lycosa (from the Greek for "wolf") is the name of this visitor. Its temporary home is probably under the floorboards or down in the basement close to the chimney. We see it checking out a new addition to the woodpile, hoping for a few insects that might be hiding under the bark. He or she might have been making these forages all winter long. Most wolf spiders live much longer than one year, and ours would be foolish to give up a good home for a cold spot out in the woods or garden.

As spring approaches and nights outside are only cool, not cold, *Lycosa* goes out to the garden, departing through one of the many exits in the unmortared fieldstone of our house foundation. These spiders spend their summers in the garden or fields with others of their kind, usually beneath the many flat rocks in the scree bed.

This spider is a true hunter, purging the garden of pests throughout the summer and fall. It has exchanged the spider web for good eyesight and strong legs that move with great speed. Its fearsome head has four small eyes that look slightly down from the front of the face and a little to each side. Just above these are two larger eyes pointing straight ahead, and on the top of the head, two more look up. Thus, the wolf spider can see in four directions at once and focus on a future dinner at a distance of several inches.

After mating, the female spins an egg sac of spider silk. Once full of eggs, the sac is often as large as the spider's body, and she will carry it wherever she goes.

I usually scare a wolf spider every day while working in the scree bed and startle two more whenever I weed in the garden. They dash for cover, holding the precious bag over their heads. Later, when the eggs hatch, the young will ride about on the mother's back for a week or so before they leave the immediate area by ballooning.

The fearsome spider of folklore—the spider that could with one bite send the victim into that frenzy of uncontrolled spastic torment, the tarantula dance—is a large European wolf spider, *Lycosa tarentula*. Recent findings suggest that such dances were performed by willing peasants for tourists and that the magnitude of the bite's symptoms was in direct proportion to the fee paid for the performance.

The Harvestmen

Harvestmen, or daddy longlegs, are not true spiders. They lack a separate head (or cephalothorax) and abdomen but instead have both these parts in one body segment. They have only two eyes and no spinning glands at all. Still, they are close relatives and, because of their eight legs, are often thought of as spiders. They belong to the Phalangiidae family, with the eastern daddy longlegs being one of many species of *Leiobunum* and the brown species, *Phalangium opilio.*

Harvestmen sometimes kill tiny insects for food but usually feed on the dead, ingesting juices from overripe fruits and vegetables. Although they are found in abundance from late spring to the first killing frosts, most people see them at harvest time, hence the common name.

Adults die in autumn, although a few might overwinter in the southern regions. Their eggs, buried in the ground, hatch with the warming days of spring. The baby harvestmen are very small and take to hiding under rocks and leaves during the day. At twilight they wander about looking for food, slowly growing larger.

Although the legs are long, the harvestman usually walks with them bent in such a way that the body hovers just above the ground. Sometimes legs are lost, and three-legged individuals are often seen. The legs do not regenerate. In the fall, harvestmen may congregate, their myriad legs interlocked as they huddle in the crevice formed by two logs or in a knothole of a tree.

You may often see clusters of tiny red spots at the joints of the legs. These are tiny parasitic mites, which are also closely related to the spiders. Their relationship is akin to that described in this popular poem:

> *Little fleas have lesser fleas*
> *Upon the backs to bite them;*
> *Lesser fleas have smaller fleas,*
> *And so ad infinitum.*

THE GREAT MEDICINE SHOW

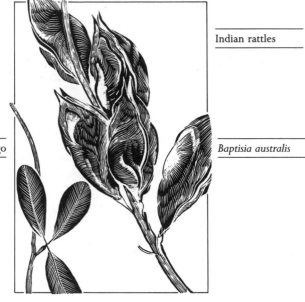

Indian rattles

Blue false indigo

Baptisia australis

I know you all have plenty on your minds. Every day unleashes new horror stories that you can do nothing about. You must grin and bear it. Remember the poem by Sam Foss (1858–1911)?

> *No financial throw volcanic*
>   *Ever yet was known to scare it;*
> *Never yet has any panic*
>   *Scared the firm of Grin and Barrett.*

Right now, as we read, ignorant man continues to burn, bulldoze, and steal from the world of plants. "What value are these plants anyway?" ask the perpetrators.

I have in our library a 1972 copy of *Potter's New Cyclopaedia of Medicinal Herbs and Preparations,* first published in England in 1907. There are more than four hundred pages of remedies. Most are as yet unproven. A few are downright dangerous. But a vast majority are still used and have proven successful. And the formulas are all derived from plants.

According to *A Field Guide to Medicinal Plants,* by Steven Foster and James A. Duke (The Peterson Field Guide Series, 1990), over 40 percent of the prescription drugs sold in the United States today contain at least one ingredient taken from nature. And if that isn't impressive enough, 25 percent of those prescription drugs have an ingredient taken from a flowering plant.

Quinine, for example, comes from the bark of the cinchona tree *(Cinchona calisaya)*; the dried leaves of the common fox-glove *(Digitalis purpurea)* are the source of digitalis, used to treat heart conditions; the rauvolfia plant *(Rauvolfia serpentina)* produces reserpine, used in tranquilizers.

More than eight hundred species of plants in North America have been or are being used to produce chemicals and compounds for treating and curing disease. The properties of many other species are as yet unknown.

Recently the *New York Times* reported that the first laboratory syntheses of a compound, ginkgolide B, could eventually lead to its widespread use in treating asthma, toxic shock, Alzheimer's disease, and various circulatory orders. Where does this compound originally come from? The leaves of the ginkgo tree *(Ginko biloba).*

Mark J. Plotkin, director of plant conservation for the World Wildlife Fund, said the synthesis of ginkgo chemistry was an important reminder of the value of plants in human medicine and of the need to intensify the study and preservation of the world's flora.

Before the New World was discovered by the Europeans, its native cultures had used medications taken from hundreds of the indigenous trees and wildflowers in a complex tradition of medicine. Bark from white willow *(Salix alba)*, which contains salicin, a precursor to aspirin, was chewed to treat headaches . . . the powdered root of white lettuce *(Prenanthes alba)* was added to a new mother's food to stimulate milk flow after childbirth . . . the catalog of such remedies shows that the first Americans were in many ways far more sophisticated than today's citizens who persist in buying diet pills from TV hucksters.

Four wildflowers should be in every garden devoted to medicinal plants. They also have been and are used in research and the preparation of drugs: blue false indigo, cohosh, the passionflower, and the purple coneflower.

BLUE FALSE INDIGO

I still remember many of the plants that grew in our first formal garden. Three of the plants that stood in a row on top of the bank were false indigos, and they did a great job of holding the soil. They looked down on slopes of myrtle and hay-scented ferns, all leading down to our red Japanese maple. They never ceased to amaze, from the flowers of late spring to the seedpods (known as Indian rattles) of fall.

Baptisias are native Americans, first reported to commerce in 1758. The botanical name is *Baptisia australis*. The genus is derived from *bapto*, "to dye"—and thereby hangs a tale—and *australis*, "of the south," refers to the southern part of North America, not the continent Australia.

In colonial times everyone thought these plants would substitute for indigo, the blue dye obtained from species of *Indigo-*

fera. Fortunes were going to be made. Unfortunately, the color from *Baptisia* is not fast, and many fortunes were lost.

But baptisias have other uses. The American Indians used hot tea made from the root as an emetic and purgative, and they drank a cold tea to stop vomiting. When held in the mouth, the liquid relieved toothaches. It was used to treat rheumatism, too, and an ointment made from boiling down the liquid decoction was applied to inflamed tumors and ulcers. Today the plant is being researched as a potential stimulant of the immune system, but users are warned that extracts from the plant are considerd potentially toxic.

Because they are legumes, baptisias will grow moderately well even in poor soil and are excellent plants for holding banks of earth and preventing erosion.

This is a plant that needs planning before planting. The root system becomes so extensive that old plants are not easily moved. If you're using seedlings, set them out by the second spring. In time, each will cover an area of several feet with their graceful foliage.

Baptisia will adapt to filtered shade, but the growth will not be as generous; it's best to provide full sun and a well-drained, acid soil. They are hardy to USDA Zone 4.

In the fall the foliage will turn coal black with frost and becomes especially striking when planted with goldenrods and little bluestem ornamental grasses.

To save the seedpods, cut them on long stems in early fall before they become too weathered. Place them upright in a dry, well-ventilated spot until needed. The popular name of Indian rattle is well deserved. Thoreau notes in a February entry of his journal,

> As I stood by Eagle Field wall, I heard a fine
> rattling sound, produced by the wind on some dry

weeds at my elbow. It was occasioned by the wind rattling the fine seeds in those pods of the indigo-weed which were still closed–like a small Indian's calabash.

COHOSH

The Indians called it cohosh. The settlers called it fairy-candle for the narrow racemes of white flowers. The botanical name *Cimicifuga racemosa* comes from *cimex,* Latin for "bug," and *fugare,* "to flee"–hence its other common name, bugbane. Both refer to the supposed insect-repellent smell of the flowers. The odor is rather rank but nothing to cause anyone to run scream-ing from the garden.

The most important part of cohosh is the root. *Potter's New Cyclopaedia* describes the rhizome with great attention to detail, including the fact that roots in transverse section reveal woody tissue in the shape of a Maltese cross.

The taste is described as being bitter and acrid and rather astringent with a very disagreeable odor. The 1898 *British Phar-mocopea* lists the dosage in drops for its use in a tincture (the sap is insoluble in water and must be dissolved in pure or diluted spirits or wine), with the warning that overdoses pro-duce nausea and vomiting. Applied topically, it is listed as a bug repellent.

Among its chemicals are glycosides actaeine, cimicifugin, racemosin, estrogen substances, triterpenes, isoferulic acid, and tannin. According to *A Field Guide to Medicinal Plants,* cohosh preparations are used for bronchitis, chorea, fevers, nervous disorders, lumbago, menstrual irregularities, rheumatism, and snakebites (which accounts for another common name, black snakeroot). Women are warned not to use any part of cohosh during pregnancy.

The flowers are numerous and small, with no petals, and the sepals fall away as they open. The lowermost flowers open first. Soon the top foot of the six- to eight-foot stalk is covered with clusters of glistening stamens, like shining, silvery white filaments. The toothed leaves, borne near the ground, are large and divided. Seedpods form and make a curious rattling sound, hence yet another common name, rattletop.

Where soil is continually moist, cimicifugas will take some sun in the North, but south of Pennsylvania they are best left to shady sites with just a touch of sun in morning or late afternoon. The soil needs a hint of humus and should be on the acid side. Once planted, they can be left alone for years. Both wild species spread seed about, so there should never be a lack of plants. They are hardy to USDA Zone 4.

Cimicifuga americana is the shorter of the two American species, with flower stalks to six feet. *C. racemosa* can reach eight feet, depending on soil and moisture. 'Brunette' is a new cultivar with bronzy brown foliage that grows to five feet. 'Atropurpurea' only reaches three feet. A variety *cordifolia* has fewer leaves.

Many native American plants, especially from the east coast, have counterparts in Japan. Three Japanese species are now on the nursery market. *Cimicifuga dahurica* blooms on five-foot stalks, and *C. japonica* 'Acerina' blooms in July on three-foot stalks. *C. simplex* blooms the latest of all, often well into October. Two cultivars are usually available: 'Braunlaub' with brown leaves, and 'White Pearl', whose unopened buds look like a pearl necklace.

A shaded walkway between our garden and the garden next door is edged on the higher side with a long line of *Cimicifuga americana*. Its six-foot spires all bloom at the end of August well into September and delight everyone who walks by. Years ago in our old country garden I planted one *C. racemosa* so that its eight-foot flower stalk wound its way through the branches of a Japanese maple; the evening sun would cast red shades on the white flowers. Graham Stuart Thomas, one of England's greatest plantsmen, rates *C. racemosa* not only a truly good garden plant but also one of exceptional beauty. I agree.

PASSIONFLOWER

More than 350 members of the passionflower family are native to both the Old World and the New, but most are found in tropical America. Early in the 1600s, a Catholic friar, Emanuele Villegas, while wandering through Mexico became the first recorded European to see the plant in bloom. In 1610 he presented a drawing of the blossom to the Roman theologian Giacomo Bosio, who immediately imbued it with religious symbolism, calling it

> the most extraordinary representation of the Cross Triumphant ever discovered in field or forest. The flower contains within itself not only the Savior's Cross but also the symbols of His Passion.

The flower described in the drawing is most likely *Passiflora incarnata (passio* is "suffering," and *flor-,* "flower"), a native plant found in the southern United States and northern Mexico. It was called maypop or maracock by the Algonquin Indians.

Bosio was so excited by the admittedly stylized drawing that he wrote the following:

> The filaments which surmount [the petals] resemble a fringe spattered with blood, thus seeming to represent the flail with which Christ was scourged. The column at which He was scourged rises from the center of the flower, the three nails with which He was nailed to the Cross are above it, and the column is surrounded by the Crown of Thorns. At the flower's exact center . . . there is a yellow zone bearing five blood-colored marks symbolic of the

Five Wounds inflicted on Our Lord . . . Surrounding these elements is a kind of violet-colored nimbus composed of 72 filaments that correspond to the number of spines in the Crown of Thorns. The plant's numerous and attractive leaves are shaped like a lance-head, and remind us of the Lance of Longinus which pierced the Saviour's side. Their undersurface is marked with flecks of white which symbolized Judas' thirty pieces of silver.

Bosio forgot to note that the five petals and five sepals make up ten of the apostles (omitting Peter and Judas), that the sepals remaining on the vine after the flower falls are the Trinity, and that the whips of persecution are seen in the coiling tendrils of the vine.

Maypops grow from Virginia to Florida and west to Missouri and Texas. And their importance in producing drugs far outweighs their religious significance.

The American Indians used the roots to treat boils, cuts and abrasions, earaches, and inflammations in general. They also used solutions as antispasmotics and as sedatives for neuralgia, epilepsy, painful menses, general restlessness, insomnia, and believe it or not, tension headaches—life in colonial America wasn't always as calm as people want to believe it was.

Contemporary research shows that extracts of the passionflower are mildly sedative and useful in reducing blood pressure, increasing respiratory rates, and decreasing motor activity. Contemporary users are warned that extracts from this plant are harmful in large amounts; nevertheless the fruits are often used to make a delicious jam.

The strong-growing vines are hardy to USDA Zone 6, where they die down to the ground each winter. They need well-drained but moist garden soil in full sun.

Sow fresh seed in the spring. Germination takes about a

month, and plants should flower in their second year. They can also be propagated from stem cuttings during the spring and summer.

Flowers develop on the new growth, so prune the vine once a year while it is dormant, cutting back one third of the canes and stopping just above a lateral bud.

PURPLE CONEFLOWER

The purple coneflower, *Echinacea purpurea*, is another native American with medicinal properties. Its botanical name comes from *echinos*, "hedgehog," since the receptacle (the plant part that holds the flower) is prickly.

The cone-shaped and prickly heads of bronzy brown are surrounded by petals (really ray flowers) that open on the horizontal but soon droop (the botanical term for such inclination is *reflexed*). Colors are varying shades of rose-purple, and flowers bloom on very stout stalks from two to four feet high, often continuing until cut down by a hard frost. The simple and alternate leaves are very rough to the touch.

The coneflowers are important ingredients of pharmaceutical compounds, especially in Europe. In addition to essential oils, the plants contain glycosice echinacoside, echinaceine, resin, inulin, betaine, and phenolic acid.

More than two hundred preparations are manufactured from coneflowers, making them one of the stars on the pharmaceutical horizon. These include extracts for treating wounds, herpes sores, and throat infections. Present research centers on stimulation of nonspecific defense mechanisms.

Coneflowers are especially beautiful when massed in the wildflower garden. In fact, the more, the better. They are excellent cut flowers and are able to withstand drought. Remember to deadhead them for prolonged blooming.

If grown from seed, coneflowers take about a year in the garden to develop into a large clump, but if started early, they will bloom the first summer. Time divisions for early spring, and pot them up for a few weeks until a new root system develops, because plants resent moving. Once in place, they should not be disturbed for several years. They are hardy to USDA Zone 4.

Echinacea purpurea is the plant usually offered by nurseries and seed houses. John Banister, an English naturalist, sent the first seeds from America to the Oxford Botanic Garden sometime in the mid-1680s. 'Magnus' has broad, nonreflexed petals of rose pink on thirty-six-inch stems, 'Bright Star' has maroon flowers on thirty-inch stems, 'The King' has large blooms of carmine red on forty-inch stems, and 'White Swan' has white flowers on thirty-inch stems.

For a plant of shorter stature, look for the narrow-leaved coneflower *(E. angustifolia),* whose stems are about twenty inches tall and bear flowers with shorter rays.

The pale purple coneflower *(E. pallida)* has narrow, reflexed petals on three- to five-foot stalks and a long taproot that enables it to survive most contingencies in the garden. Native Americans of the northern Great Plains used it more than any other plant to treat ailments.

So remember that the continual drive to open new lands for development – all done in the name of progress – could very well lead to the demise of the one plant that could prevent tooth decay or even cure the common cold.

JANET'S ROCK

Dicranum
longifolium

Bartramia
pomiformis

Andrea petrophila

Hylocomnium
triquetrum

There is a rock in Janet's garden that was brought there by the last glacier as it retreated through the Catskill Mountains some ten thousand years ago. The rock is eight feet long and close to eight feet wide on the west side, tapering to two feet wide on the east side. This rock is like an iceberg: Only 10 percent is above ground. It's the kind of rock that demands a capital R. When Janet and Tom built their home, the man who ran the earth-moving equipment said that if they could live with the Rock, they should. Blasting would be the only way to make an impact on it, and the results of a blast—especially with the house only fifteen feet away—were at best uncertain.

Janet had always been fond of wildflowers and since the late

1940s had treasured a well-worn copy of a 1915 book, *Flower Guide for Wild Flowers East of the Rockies*, by Chester A. Reed. Opposite the title page is an oval photograph of a very small girl in a gingham dress. She's wearing a large, flouncy sunbonnet and picking oxeye daisies in a field. It's titled "Her First Lesson in Botany."

Janet decided that living with the Rock was the best choice. "It will be a moss, lichen, and whatever-else-happens-to-show-up garden," she said.

One August weekend under a Payne's gray sky with a light, drizzling rain—the first rain we'd had in weeks—Janet and I took inventory of the inhabitants of the Rock. Except for a few choice clumps of lichens and mosses brought back from nature walks on other parts of their property, everything growing on the Rock had started on its own.

The Rock itself is surrounded by old daffodils (bulbs brought from fifty-year-old plants at Janet's home in Indiana), some wild irises *(Iris versicolor)*, white crocuses (also from Indiana), a large clump of lady fern *(Athyrium filix-femina)*, a trailing variety of bouncing Bet *(Saponaria ocymoides)*, and various wild grasses of short stature.

Almost at the Rock's center and highest point, a six-year-old white pine seedling *(Pinus strobus)* stretched ten inches into the air. The roots were lost in a large clump of reindeer moss. The little pine has dwarfed naturally because the Rock offers little soil, and each year's candles are never more than an inch long. It is the Rock's own bonsai.

Mosses and Lichens

By far the largest number of plants on the Rock are mosses, small green plants that usually prefer shade. Back in 1907, Nina L. Marshall wrote the following paean to mosses in *Mosses and Lichens:*

The blackened embers of the picnic fire are hidden with golden cord-mosses and the roadsides in the woods and the slopes to the lake are carpeted with sturdy hairy-caps. The crumbling roofs of deserted cottages and the unused wellsweep and old oaken bucket are decorated with soft tufts of green.

Most mosses need shade. Because they have poorly developed water-distribution systems, the hot sun can dry them out before water can reach thirsty cells. Hair-cap moss will grow in open fields, but in that environment the grass provides some protection and helps collect and then channel the morning dews to the mosses below. Mosses fold up their leaves when dry, markedly changing their appearance. But when water comes again, individual cells quickly swell and the mosses revert to normal size.

Mosses reproduce by releasing spores from artful containers called *peristomes.* Looking at various peristomes – for each genus has a design all its own – is like looking at a Paul Klee etching of Turkish minarets. These fanciful capsules are edged with teeth that vary in number from four to sixty-four, always in multiples of four. When damp, the teeth are closed tightly together; when dry, they open up and the spores are shaken to the winds like salt cast from a saltcellar. Peristomes have been called some of the most beautifully sculptured forms in nature.

When a spore lands in a favorable spot, it opens, and the single cell begins to form a thread (called *protonema)* and thin roots *(rhizoids).* Soon it becomes a mature *gametophyte* and forms an *archegonia* (which produces eggs) and an *antheridia* (which produces sperm). When an egg is fertilized, it becomes a *sporophyte,* which upon maturation produces spores – and the cycle begins again.

Lichens are a different story. These relatively simple plants are a careful combination of green algae and colorless fungi that live only in areas where the air is pure and unsullied by pollution. Their partnership is called symbiosis: The fungi provide a house for the algae, which in turn manufacture food like any other green plant—by making nutrients from water and air, using the power of the sun.

Lichens provide food for small insects and larger mammals. In the Arctic, reindeer moss (really a lichen) is the principal diet of caribou during harsh winters; in the Northeast, deer often survive by feeding on tree lichens when no other food is available. Lichens are intolerant of sulphur dioxide and other impurities of city air. Only a few cities in America can harbor them. A few are found in the suburbs, but most lichens prefer the rural life.

Nina Marshall described lichens thus:

A small sisterhood of plodding lichens
Wrought on the rock; the sun, the wind and rain,
Helping them gladly, till each fissure filled—

Reproduction for lichens is by asexual means. New plants are simply formed from broken pieces of the old. Lichens also produce fruiting bodies in many colors on top of their tiny branches, and these, too, are often fanciful in design. Although spores are produced, no one has ever successfully grown new lichens by germinating these spores. The action of sexual reproduction for lichens is especially complicated. Botanists know that the fungal spore must find a compatible alga to join it before a lichen is produced, but they have no idea how this is accomplished in nature.

Both lichens and mosses can exist on bare rock. By chemical means they produce food. By mechanical means they remove tiny pieces of hard rock, threading their rhizoids into microscopic pores in the rock's surface, gaining trace elements for nutrition and slowly, over eons, making soil. Even airborne dust from mountain roads and trails is trapped by the tiny hornlike projections of the lichens and the leaves of the mosses, eventually to combine with old crumpled and dehydrated plants to form new accumulations of dirt. Given enough time, the little white pine will someday find soil on the top of Janet's Rock.

AN INVENTORY OF THE ROCK

Upon the Rock itself that day, rooted in its crevices and crannies, were nine species of moss; eleven species of lichen; one sedge (unidentified); a bit of ground ivy *(Glecoma hederacea)*; some partridge berry *(Mitchella repens)*; two tiny meadow puffballs *(Lycoperdon pratense)*; five tiny mushrooms, known as the little wheel Marasmius *(Marasmius rotula),* each having one-and-a-half-inch-wide caps on thin two-inch stems; plus three baby crickets, a few ants, one small brown toad, and two efts (the land-locked stage of the immature eastern salamander).

Despite the excitement of finding such a variety of living things, we returned to the mosses and lichens. Using a few snippets of the mosses, previous knowledge of the lichens, plus three nature field guides, we identified all that we found on Janet's Rock.

The ostrich-plume feather moss *(Hypnum crista-castrensis)* looks like a miniature example of its namesake, since the plants have bright yellow-green plumes. The word *hypnum* is Greek and suggests that these mosses were once helpful in promoting sleep; the species name refers to the castle shape of the branches. The spore capsules are large, curved, and held on the horizontal. This moss is common in mountainous regions on soil and rotten wood.

The tiny cedar moss *(Thuidium delicatulum)* received both its botanical and its common name because of its close resemblance to a cedar tree in miniature, *thuidium* being derived from an ancient Greek name for some resin-bearing evergreen.

This moss was well known to Linnaeus, the great Swedish botanist who worked out the Latin system of naming plants. He called it *delicatulum* in recognition of its dainty appearance. It enjoys damp, shady places and runs over stones, earth, and rotting logs.

Apple moss *(Bartramia pomiformis)* gets its species name, "in the shape of an apple," because the plant's tiny spore case indeed looks like a little apple, *pomum.* Thirteen species are found in North America, usually growing in rock clefts. It was named in honor of John Bartram (1699–1777), the great American botanist from Pennsylvania.

The fork moss *(Dicranum longifolium)* is named after a Greek word for flesh-hook or fork; its spore case bears a menacing formation of teeth. The species name refers to the very long leaves. It is among sixty-five species in North America; at the turn of the century, six were found within the limits of New York City. American Indians called the fork moss "woman's heads" because when trampled underfoot it springs right up again, a not-so-subtle reference to the indomitable spirit of woman. Fork moss grows only in high-altitude, rocky regions, sometimes at the base of trees.

Pincushion mosses *(Leucobryum longifolium)* look so much like pincushions that little imagination was needed for the name. The genus name is Greek for "white moss," referring to the pallid green, unusual among mosses. Because the chlorophyll-containing cells are surrounded by larger transparent cells, specially constituted to carry water and to protect the small cells from heat, they appear to be pale green.

The stone-loving andreaea *(Andreaea petrophila)* grows on granite or slate rocks in shady, damp places. It is among the first colonizers to make such inhospitable surfaces home for life. The genus is named in honor of the German botanist G. R. Andreae. The species name comes from *petra*, Greek for rock.

Hair-cap moss *(Polytrichum commune)* has been known and

watched since ancient Greece. Pliny called it "golden maiden-hair" because of the golden gloss the leaves exhibit when dry. In the grand tradition of marketing, these mosses were once used to make a rinse for women's hair because the veils on the spore capsules were said to resemble a lady's tresses—hence the common name. A century ago many souvenir pillows (decorated with shining beads and winsome fringes) from exotic places like Niagara Falls or Sioux City were filled with hair-cap moss in lieu of the more expensive feathers. These mosses were once dedicated to Venus and then to the Virgin Mary and were the first plants to be recognized by early botanists as not having true flowers. The genus name is from *poly*, "many," and *trichum*, "hair."

The arched feather moss *(Hypnum splendens)* is a beautiful combination of gold and green leaves on reddish stems. This splendid plant is common on rocks in the deep woods and on fallen stumps and rotting logs. Miss Marshall wrote of them,

> *Glittering with yellow, red and green,*
> *As o'er the moss, with playful glide,*
> *The sunbeams dance from side to side.*

The last moss on Janet's Rock has the most romantic common name of all: the triangular wood-reveler—and that's exactly what the genus means in Greek. *Hylocomnium triquetrum* grows only on wood with a luxuriant delight that led to the term, *reveler*, as named by one William Philipp Schimper, who was no slouch when it came to nomenclature. The stems are triangular. And as Miss Marshall noted,

> *The moss upon the forest bark*
> *Was polestar when the night was dark.*

The lichens are not as soft and comfortable looking as the

mosses, but they make up for it in their more fanciful shapes and subtle colors. Bring a bit of any species of lichen into good light, and with a clean hand lens let your eye wander around the miniature landscape of another world.

British soldiers *(Cladonia cristatella)* are named in honor of the redcoats in the Revolutionary War. After a rain, their red tips (really another type of spore case) glow in the sunlight and, though only an inch tall, can be seen for yards. Their favorite place of attachment is an old piece of dead wood. *Cladonia* refers to their branchlike pattern of growth.

The goblet lichens *(Cladonia pyxidata)* look like tiny cups made to hold beer or wine for an elf convention. The species is from the word for a small box. There is a painting by Thomas Cole (1801–1848), the American landscape artist of the Hudson River School, called "Titan's Goblet." The painting shows a stone goblet so large that a tiny sailboat can be seen arrowing through the waves as thin sprays of water drip over the edge and fade into the distance; the cup is patterned after the goblet lichen.

Reindeer mosses *(Cladonia rangiferina)* grow into a tangle of interlocking threads as thick as the hair on a bear's back. They are often ashy white or tinged with light green. We found two kinds on Janet's Rock, one smaller and more tightly packed and known as *C. rangiferina* var. *alpestris. Rangiferina,* from the French, refers to the genus for reindeer and caribou.

Fringed cladonia *(Cladonia fimbriata)* grows into tiny structures. The goblet-shaped branches are tipped with fringe, hence the species name, from Latin for "fringe." It usually grows directly on the soil.

The last of the cladonias, *C. verticillata,* a species with no common name, bears little branches on top, arranged like spokes on a wheel. The species name means "in a whorled manner."

The Rock is also home to four of the so-called crustose

lichens. These plants are so flat and stick so closely to the surface that they appear to be extensions of rock rather than anything living.

Physicia stellaris forms light gray rosettes dotted with tiny black spore cases that look like tiny craters on the moon; the generic name is Greek for "blister." The edges are wavy and wrinkled, forming an almost perfect circle, hence the Latin *stellaris* because they resemble the rays of a star.

Janet's Rock doesn't interest everyone. To appreciate it, you must delight in the small and shun bravado.

MOTH AND FLANNEL MULLEINS

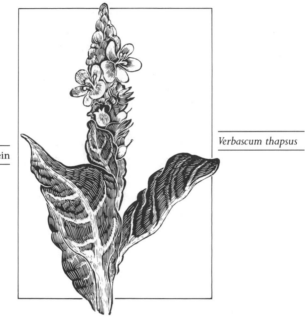

Common mullein

Verbascum thapsus

My father used to joke a lot. If my mother happened to remark that Tallulah Bankhead was very funny on "The Big Show," my father would turn to her and say, "Ah, she was brilliant—as brilliant as a dead mackerel lying on the beach in the moonlight." Then he'd chuckle, and my mother would say, "Oh, Harry."

He loved to work in a mention of the Apple Sisters, Cora and Seedy. I always think of them when I confront the common wild mulleins, moth and flannel.

The mulleins belong to the genus *Verbascum,* the ancient Roman name for these plants applied by Pliny. In fact, some wordsmiths believe that this is a corruption of *barbascum,* meaning "with beards," referring to the hairy texture of the leaves. Mullein itself is the Old French *moleine* and derives from the Latin *mollis,* "soft."

Common mullein, or *Verbascum thapsus,* is a biennial producing only rosettes of woolly leaves the first year. Not until the heat of the following August does it send up the towering floral stalks covered with one-inch yellow flowers that bear orange woolly anthers. Often called flannel plant, velvet plant, great torch plant, and Aaron's rod, flannel mullein is better known than moth mullein. The species name refers to the island of Thapsos, the plant's native land. Other folk names include donkey's ear, bunny's ears, cow's ear, flannel petticoats, and poor man's flannel. You have only to touch the leaves to know the reason for these nicknames. If examined under a hand lens, the hairs turn out to be branched like tiny trees.

The Romans called it candelaria, and the ladies used the blossoms steeped in lye for a yellow hair dye. People picked the ripened floral stems, often up to seven feet tall, dipped them in melted suet, and used them to light funeral processions. Imagine: The plant that blooms in the empty field next to your nearest mall was once used to light a mausoleum for the internment of a Roman real estate broker or developer. The Greeks were not as flamboyant and cut the leaves into strips for lamp wicks.

Since mulleins abound in areas with poor, dry soil where they are exposed to winds, sun, and cold, the hairs are a definite protection.

Although it's sometimes called American velvet plant, the flannel mullein is an import. It may have been brought over intentionally with other herbs by the settlers, or it may be here by accident. The English and French have always been a frugal lot. Rather than send valuable cargo to the New World, they loaded the holds with just plain dirt so that the ships sailing west would ride low in the water. After arriving in America, sailors unloaded the dirt and threw it all over the Eastern seaboard. The weed seeds within went forth.

Mullein is magic. Ulysses used a mullein stalk from the gods, given to him by Mercury, for defense against Circe – and he lived to tell the tale. According to Cockaye's book *Leechdoms, Wortcunning, and Starcraft of Early England* (note leechdoms and pause – or consider this a name for a new law firm),

> If a man beareth with him one twig of this wort,
> he will not be terrified with any awe, nor will a wild
> beast hurt him; or any evil coming near.

Mullein has a long medicinal history. The part of the plant used is the yellow corolla or flower proper. But leaves and flowers were both part of an infusion administered for pulmonary complaints.

Mullein has also been made into a poultice for ulcers, tumors, piles, and kidney infections. Flowers soaked in mineral oil were used as drops for earaches. The juice of flowers and leaves was used to remove warts but – in the continual contradictions of folk medicine – was ineffectual against smooth warts.

And shades of *The Creature from the Black Lagoon*, fish poachers would cast the seeds on water to numb the fish, a practice that is successful because the leaves contain rotenone. Could the leaves be a possible source for producing an insecticide?

Of course, the problem with mullein for the formal garden is the blooming of the flowers. Rather than opening from the top or perhaps from the bottom, they choose to open at odd places along the stem. But they are unsurpassed for the stems alone.

When bees alight on the five stamens, they settle on the longer bottom two–thus dusting their undersides with pollen–while taking hold of the three shorter ones for nectar. Then at the next blossom, their bellies are cleaned when going in, and they pick up more when backing out.

There are many cultivated mulleins for the formal border, but a group of the common mulleins towering against either the sky or arranged in front of a wooded backdrop is a welcome addition to the wild garden. Once they are established, you will have the towering stems every summer. If unwanted, the rosettes are easily removed during their first year.

Verbascum blattaria, or moth mullein, is another biennial (rarely an annual) that is much the gentler sister. Rumor says that this plant will repel cockroaches, or *blatta,* hence the species name. If that's true, I'm sure big-city apartment dwellers would grow it on windowsills instead of calling in the exterminator.

The slender stems can reach to six feet but are usually shorter. The simple smooth leaves are paper napkins compared with the turkish toweling of the previous plant. Pretty flowers open from below. They are usually yellow (occasionally white) and five-parted, and the stamens are covered with violet woolly filaments dotted with orange pollen.

When packing away winter woolens, colonial women used this plant to repel clothes moths. But the common name is more likely from the look of the blossoms.

FRAGRANT PATHWAYS
OF THE MOUNTAINS

Sweet fern

*Comptonia
peregrina*

Karl L. Brooks, in his book *A Catskill Flora and Economic Botany,*
lists sweetfern as *Comptonia peregrina,* crediting the name to
Emerson in 1878.

In 1963 edition of *The New Britton and Brown Illustrated
Flora of the Northeastern United States and Adjacent Canada* lists
the sweetfern as belonging to the genus *Myrica* (an ancient
Greek name for a fragrant plant). But in an introductory pas-
sage, the writer remarks that because of some interesting botan-

ical characteristics, sweetfern may also be called *Comptonia asplenifolia.*

Hortus Third lists this plant as one species of the genus *Comptonia* with two forms: the species *peregrina* and a variety with less pubescent leaves and smaller catkins known as var. *asplenifolia.*

So let us call the plant by the old name of *Comptonia,* a name in honor of Henry Compton (1632–1713), once the Bishop of London, a gentleman who was a patron of botany and imported many uncommon and rare plants to his garden. *Peregrina* means "foreign, traveling," referring to the wandering habit of this plant.

Common names are many and include fern-gale, shrubby-fern, meadow-fern, sweet-bush, sweet-ferry, spleenwort-bush, Canada sweet-gale, and fernwort.

The plant's range is wide. It grows from Nova Scotia to Saskatchewan, then south to North Carolina and Georgia and west to Illinois and Minnesota. Its habitat is open, sterile hillsides, roadsides, waste places, and pastures—in fact, any place where the soil is rough, stony, dry, and well-drained.

The books describe it as a low deciduous shrub (it has no relationship to ferns), usually three to four feet high with fernlike leaves that exude a pleasant spicy fragrance when crushed. The plants are monoecious (they bear male catkins and globular female flower heads on the same plant). The eventual fruits are burrlike and contain nutlets.

In his 1960 book *Using Wayside Plants,* Nelson Coon (a gentleman garden writer both knowledgeable and delightful), wrote of sweetfern,

> Although not now highly rated for any medicinal
> properties, at one time considerable use was made of
> a decoction of the leaves for diseases requiring medi-

cine of an astringent quality, considerable evidence being given of its value in cases of diarrhea.

The aromatic leaves and flowers were used during the Revolutionary War to prepare a tea substitute. The plant was considered quite palatable; children of long ago would even nibble on the young nutlets.

I have problems though, with the words *quite palatable.* I remember when *conservation* was a buzzword–the first time around–and Euell Gibbons wrote books advising us to eat naturally (and did a number of TV commercials for breakfast cereals). Those of us who had moved to the countryside (but still communicated with Manhattan) thought it a great idea; those who had lived their lives on the farm did not. But two or three dinners built around soup made from lichens or boiled cattail roots taught us newcomers what *quite palatable* implies. Yes, if you are hungry and the wolves are howling at the door, these foods will get you by. But tasty cuisine they are not.

I suggest growing the plant not for tea but as an attractive shrub that will thrive where other plants do not. The leaves resemble that tropical houseplant the false aralia *(Dizygotheca elegantissima),* and the plants should be set along the edge of a path so that every time you walk by in the heat of summer, you can pick a leaf and smell the sweet smells of the woods and mountains long, long ago.

DRACULA'S CLOCK

Evening primrose   *Oenothera biennis*

I, for one, will be delighted when architectural styles change and the postmodern phase phases itself out. Mall after mall and office after office, everything new looks alike. Whether in Toledo or Kansas City, all the building fronts look like downtown Karnak (one mile east of Luxor) about three thousand years into Egyptian civilization.

Well, you ask, what do postmodern buildings have to do with wildflowers? Not much after they are built. But all those malls, all those blacktopped parking lots, all those round-eyed buildings are covering up fields and waste places that were once home to countless plants, both good and bad—one of the good plants being the evening primrose.

There are many evening primroses. Some, like *Oenothera biennis*, are true night-bloomers. Others are day-bloomers, known as sundrops. In fact dozens of them, all wildflowers, stretch across the country from Colorado and the deserts of the Southwest to the East Coast. Both types have flowers with eight stamens, and all but one species have four narrow stigmas, crosslike, at the tip of the style.

NIGHT-BLOOMERS

These four-petaled flowers live by Dracula's clock: By day, blossoms both new and old are tightly closed and look as if they belong in so-called waste places where, in fact, they abound. Their bedraggled petals, their chins upon the leaves, appear worn out by the activities of the night before. Then as the sun sets, fresh buds quickly open to the evening, and soon the plant is glowing with a mildly incandescent sulfur-yellow, the combined effect of dozens of fragrant flowers.

Large plants growing where conditions are favorable often reach a height of five feet, but those along the roadsides are usually shorter. The stems are strong, bearing alternate, lance-shaped leaves on the way up and clusters of unopened buds, opening flowers, wilted flowers, and near-bursting seedpods, all crowded together in a nest of the willowlike leaves.

The genus *Oenothera* is from the Greek words *oinos*, "wine," and *thera*, "to hunt." The evening primrose has no connection with wine (or looking for it), but when first named, it was confused with another genus of plant whose roots possess the aroma of wine. This particular primrose is a biennial. The first year it produces symmetrical rosettes of leaves with long taproots, and the second year it flowers.

William Robinson, writing in his *The Wild Garden*, calls the oenotheras "among the handsomest of hardy flowers . . . readily naturalized in any soil." But he warns that because of their boldness they are best suited for "shrubberies, copses, and the like," best sown in an out-of-the-way spot. The plants often cover empty lots in London, just as they take root in vacant lots in American cities.

Many evening primroses have a place in our garden, both day- and night-bloomers. But there has always been a spot for a large plant of *Oenothera biennis*: good soil in full sun where the garden proper met the wild garden. Between the open glow of dusk and the pitch black of night, there is a short time on summer nights — ten minutes at most — when the atmosphere takes on a luminous quality, magnifying that primrose yellow; that is the time when this plant is at its best.

And it's the busiest time, too. For soon after four o'clock in the afternoon, the sphinx moth (often mistaken for a humming-bird) is up and flying about. Then as dusk deepens and the fragrance of the primrose increases, the moths cease fluttering and hone in on their search for nectar. They are more harmless than the typical children of the night, interested only in sap, not blood. And since the tubes of the flowers are very long, only the tongue of the hawkmoth can reach to the bottom, draining the very last drop.

William Jacob Holland, one of America's foremost lepidop-terists, wrote the following in *The Moth Book* (first published in 1903):

> Among the insects thousands and tens of thou-sands of species are nocturnal. This is true of a great majority of moths. When the hour of dusk ap-proaches stand by a bed of evening primroses, and, as the great yellow blossoms suddenly open, watch the hawkmoths coming as swiftly as meteors through the air, hovering for an instant over this blossom, probing into the sweet depths of another, and then dashing off again so quickly that the eye cannot follow them.

He then described a great bed of these flowers on a bluff in Yokohama and remembered how, as the light began to fade on the distant top of Mount Fuji, one O-Chi-san held a Japanese lantern aloft to help net hawkmoths flying to the spot.

"Ah! those nights in Japan! Can I ever forget them?" he wrote.

In addition to the biennial evening primrose, our garden has the more demure and low-growing perennial known as the Missouri evening primrose *(Oenothera missouriensis)*. Sometimes erect but more often creeping, this lovely flower is best planted in well-drained soil with plenty of rocks to tumble over. The buds are spotted with red, and the showy yellow flowers – often four inches wide – open with the slow moves of a desert cactus flower in a Disney nature film. After blooming they form large seedpods. A stunning cultivar called 'Greencourt Lemon' is suited not only for the best of the wild garden but for the perennial border as well – and it's open most of the day.

American Indians used a root tea of *Oenothera biennias* to treat obesity. The Indians also used it for bowel pains and rubbed the liquid on sore muscles to give athletes strength. Recent medical research indicates that oil from the seed might be useful in treating metabolic disorders and alcoholism. Since evening primrose oil is a natural source of essential fatty acids like gamma-linolenic acid, various preparations are found in every health food store. Our local store manager told me the oil is used to treat PMS and to reduce imflammations due to arthritis.

One last thing to cover with the evening primrose concerns the Dutch botanist Hugo de Vries (1848–1935). In 1901 de Vries published his monumental study *Die Mutationstheorie* in which he formulated the idea that evolution occurs through sudden mutations rather than through a series of gradual changes. His theories were based on a wide knowledge of plant behavior but centered on his backyard garden and a species of evening primrose, *Oenothera lamarckiana*. Now known as *O. erythrosepala,* this primrose was originally named for Jean Baptiste Lamarck, a French naturalist who lost out to Darwin in the evolutionary sweepstakes.

De Vries found a clump of *lamarckiana* growing in an abandoned site at Hilversum in Holland and noticed two obvious variations. He dug up all three plants and brought them home to his garden, where he studied these and other mutations, noting that they bred true generation after generation. He thought they were new species – although today they would be cultivars – and at the same time rediscovered Mendel's laws of heredity that were based on garden peas (for which de Vries gave Mendel full credit).

SUNDROPS

A sloping bank in front of our old farmhouse is covered with wild daylilies, and between the lilies and the lawn is a long, narrow bed of sundrops. Memories come and go, but I suspect that the sight and smell of a summer garden after a morning rain will always remind me of these bright, golden yellow flowers. If evening primroses are flowers of the night, then sundrops are the ones that throw open the secrets of the dark to the knowing glare of day.

The plants have simple leaves and are easily missed in the garden until coming into bud and bloom in high summer. For then the unassuming plants are topped with clusters of bright red buds and yellow-gold flowers.

The species are perfect in the wild garden and can hold their own at the edge of a meadow. For the formal garden, the cultivars are best because they have more and larger flowers, though a bed of any sundrops in bloom is as close as you can get to a pool of molten gold.

Care is minimum. Sundrops ask only for full sun and well-drained soil; dryness is no problem. Gathered in early winter, the seed heads make interesting additions to winter bouquets.

Oenothera fruticosa is the wild sundrop from the eastern United States. The flowers are about two inches across on stems one or two feet high. The basal rosettes are evergreen south of Philadelphia. Although this plant is a rapid spreader, it's easily controlled because the plants are shallow-rooted. 'Youngii-lapsley' is a cultivar that bears brighter flowers on twenty-four-inch stems.

Oenothera tetragona is often confused with the first species but has been subject to much more hybridizing. The results include 'Sonnenwende', a twenty-four-inch plant with beautiful orange-red buds that open to brilliant flowers with foliage that turns red in the fall; 'Yellow River', having two-inch flowers on eighteen-inch plants and foliage that turns a reddish mahogany in the fall; and 'Fireworks', a bright yellow on eighteen-inch plants.

THE HOGWEEDS
ARE COMING!

Giant hogweed

Heracleum mantegazzianum

In 1981 I wrote of the giant hogweed after planting seed in the wild part of our garden just to see if it lived up to its press. The plant did well but disappeared from the garden in 1984. In mid-August 1988 I wandered up to the woods behind our house and saw a giant plant blooming in the old barn foundation. It was the hogweed.

Towering above my head were flattened disks, each over a foot in diameter. All were loaded with thousands of tiny white flowers—ten thousand or more according to the *Royal Horticul-*

tural Dictionary of Gardening (a figure possibly arrived at the same way you find the number of cows in a field: count the legs and divide by four). The bees were coming from everywhere to sport among the blossoms.

The botanical name is *Heracleum mantegazzianum*, with the genus from *Heracleon*, the ancient Greek name of Hercules. Charlotte McLeod wrote a mystery entitled *The Curse of the Giant Hogweed*, an adventure in time travel in which the hero journeys back to old England and encounters the villain, this gigantic plant. She neglects to give the derivation of *mantegazzianum*. But I looked again in the R. H. S. Dictionary and found that the species was named in honor of Paolo Mantegazzi (1831–1910), an Italian anthropologist.

Hogweed was first imported from the Caucasus and the steppes of central Asia in 1893–not too long ago for what turned into a pest in many places. And like King Kong, it's often too tall for its own good. A member of the parsley family, it usually never tops twelve feet in height–though a botanist in Vancouver has reported that a plant next to his front door reached twenty feet before it bloomed.

Short or tall, this imposing plant has been grown for decoration in England for years. Unfortunately it escaped from cultivation, invading Battersea Park and other sites around London. Now it's doing the same in the States. The first infestation was reported in western New York, where it probably spread from Highland Park in Rochester, having been grown there as an ornamental since 1917.

Although the plant is statuesque and quite beautiful–and makes excellent dried flowers–it presents a problem. The stems are hollow and roughly one inch thick with each stem section up to two feet in length. All are filled with a sap that contains the chemical psoralen, which–when exposed to sunlight–produces a painful irritation known as phytophotodermatitis. This is a blistering affair. If a victim is not careful, the blisters may become infected. And following the blisters, disfiguring brown marks appear that may last for months. So if you want the flowers, cut the plants on cloudy day when the sun will not activate the sap.

The plant is usually listed as monocarpic (meaning it dies after flowering) and as a biennial (it grows leaves the first year, flowers the second, then passes from the scene). But a few references say that if the root becomes ensconced, hogweed can become perennial. Any garden soil will do but it prefers full sun.

Seeds are not always available commercially but usually Chiltern Seeds from England carries a few. Don't start this plant if you have children who won't take no for an answer—what looks like a great peashooter can be dangerous indeed.

TRASH TREES

Cut-leaf
staghorn sumac

Rhus typhina
'Laciniata'

I wish sometimes for the old days. Not that I am awash in nostalgia or truly believe that life was any better years ago, but I do feel there was more of a sense of continuity: a remembrance of things past, a sensible wish for a future, in addition to a more stable present. And the feeling of loss always comes to mind when I think of trees and the planting of trees. For putting an oak or a sycamore in the ground today takes a lot of fortitude; you've got to believe not only that you or yours will be there to see that tree in years to come but that the land will be, too.

In a society where people move from place to place to follow jobs, dreams, or just warm weather, planting formidable trees in the garden seems to be a practice now at a low ebb. Oh, sure, garden centers stock Japanese maples, a lot of dwarf fruit trees, and such. But the choice seems limited to those trees that offer fairly large root balls at a fairly large price. So let me offer three native Americans.

The three I have in mind are the staghorn sumac, the gray birch, and the trembling or quaking aspen. All three grow quickly, all have been called trash or weed trees, all are relatively short-lived, all do well in the poorest of soils (even charred), all are hardy to USDA Zone 4, and all deserve better press.

THE STAGHORN SUMAC

First cultivated in the early 1600s, the staghorn sumac *(Rhus typhina)* is a tree that has few demands. It grows so quickly that gratification gets a good turn, and though short-lived, it is quite beautiful in three seasons out of four. *Rhus* is an old Latin name for the genus; and *typhina* pertains to fever and refers to the tea made from the leaves or the densely hairy berries (really drupes), used by American Indians and by early settlers to treat fevers and sore throats. A kind of lemonade can be made from the berries, and though it's better than most survival foods, it needs so much sugar to be palatable for modern taste that regular lemonade is probably better for the system. Called a shrub or a tree, staghorn sumac reaches about thirty feet. The leaves are pinnate with eleven to thirty-one leaflets each. Though the natural range is throughout temperate eastern North America, the look is decidedly tropical.

Nurserymen usually think poorly of this tree, suggesting that it be put in only the poorest of soils and relegated to hillsides — and then only when erosion is a problem.

But our old friends the English gardeners remind us that it offers tropical leaves for shade in the summer, gloriously brilliant orange and scarlet foliage in the fall, unusual felted stems

when the leaves have gone—like the antlers of a stag in velvet—
and terminal cones of dark crimson fruits that persist throughout the winter. The hair on the branches changes from pink to
green the first year and is shed by the time the bark is about
three years old.

The wood can be used for walking sticks and inlay work.
Its green cast, streaked with orange, becomes satiny when
polished.

The most imaginative use of this tree that I have seen is in
the Wild Garden at Wave Hill, a public garden in the community of Riverdale in the Bronx. There a fifty-year-old tree has
generated a multitude of smaller trunks that have been either
naturally allowed or forcibly compelled by pruning to twist and
turn into a Brazilian bower—just above Manhattan.

We, too, have started such a bower at the side of our garden.
The largest tree—a chance seedling from the nearby field—
harbors three hanging houseplants in the summer, giving them
the filtered sunlight they prefer. Underneath is a cool and pleasant place to sit on a hot summer's day. By selective cutting of
the suckers that arise throughout May, June, and July, I am able
to plan the direction that my living house of shade will pursue.

Staghorn sumac can also be used as a living hedge. Cut its
tropical foliage to the ground in early spring and allow only a
year of growth before cutting again.

There is a very attractive cultivar called 'Laciniata' whose
individual leaflets are finely cut. It also deserves a place in the
garden.

QUAKING ASPENS

The quaking aspen is truly a tree of the troubled earth. When
we were forced to tear down a large complex of buildings that
stood in a field next to our old farmhouse, the only way to get
rid of the gigantic pile of wooden remains turned out to be

the local fire department, who came *en masse* with six-packs of beer and used the event as a training session. The pile burned for two weeks before beginning to cool down. Eventually we plowed over the remains the let the earth settle in for the winter.

The following spring the aspens sprouted. The bird- and wind-borne seeds germinated quickly in the poor soil, which the fire had effectively sterilized. The first year the seedlings were two to three feet high, and within five years we had an aspen grove.

How *Populus tremuloides* got its species name is obvious once you've seen the leaves in even the lightest of breezes. The leaves' flattened stalks allow them to sway back and forth, quaking.

Aspens are found from Labrador south to Virginia, Tennessee, and Missouri, then west to New Mexico and California. Mature trees can reach a height of forty to fifty feet with a trunk diameter of fifteen inches. They are old at twenty.

In late March, this tree is among the first to note the coming of spring when the buds green up. Then the mouse-gray catkins appear, sprouting little tufts of cotton, followed by the new leaves. Nothing is quite so beautiful as aspen leaves aquiver, backlit by the fierce gray skies preceding a mountain thunderstorm. For fall, the leaves turn a bright, clear gold.

Farmers where we lived would cut young aspens in the spring, tie the slim trunks in small bundles and pull them through the fields, for they did a neater job of breaking up the clods of soil than the larger plowshares.

The bark was used in treatments for fever and as a tonic; a tea made of the inner bark was used for venereal disease and, since the bark contains aspirinlike salicin, stomach pains.

If you have the space, use these trees in a group so that they complement each other. Nothing is more beautiful than an aspen grove at the edge of a woods or field.

THE GRAY BIRCH

The gray birch *(Betula populifolia)* is another underestimated tree. Large numbers of them grew in the abandoned fields between our garden and the woods proper. Instead of being papery white like the canoe birch, they have a chalky white bark with triangular black marks below the branches. *Betula* is the ancient name for this genus, and *populifolia* means "having leaves like a poplar"–simple and triangular. They are graceful in habit until well into old age. Often multiple trunks arise, but the unwanted can be cut. The normal height is about thirty-five feet, and the trunk diameter, one foot. The natural range is from Nova Scotia to Delaware.

Critics call attention to their tendency to bend almost to the ground under the weight of heavy snow without straightening up again. We found that if we removed the snow, they quickly returned to their original shape. Some writers have said the gray birch is a weedy poor relation of the paper birch, its only advantage being an ability to withstand city soot and smoke. To me that is enough to merit inclusion in any hall of fame. I might add what *The Tree Book,* written by Julia Ellen Rogers and published in 1914, says of the gray birch:

> Graceful and hardy ornamental tree; thrives in any soil, but rarely planted. Wood used for spools, shoe pegs, wood pulp, and fuel. Valuable nurse trees to hardwoods and conifers on land Nature is re-foresting.

Because of the gray birch's bending trunk and lowly place in the forest hierarchy–like the aspen, it appears where fires have been–tongues have wagged. But again our English friends know better, for they list it as a tree for small gardens with attractive foliage and good autumn color (golden beige), excellent when planted in a small grouping. The trees are old at fifteen years but with care will last into their twenties.

Catkin buds appear on the branches in autumn but don't bloom till very early spring; in the interval seeds provide excellent food for wildlife, including ruffed grouse and songbirds. We have also noted that deer leave these trees alone unless there is absolutely nothing else to eat.

THOSE WILD AMERICANS

Fraser's sedge   *Carex fraseri*

I've been growing ornamental grasses in our perennial border for more than seventeen years, but only recently have I started using them in the wild garden, with the proviso that they be North American wild grasses and nothing from across the seas. A foolish restriction some would say, but so far I've found the selection to get larger every year—especially if you use the seed exchanges and the mom-and-pop nurseries as your suppliers.

The beauty of the American grasses lies in their versatility. After all, they come from a vast area with climate variations from high mountain to desert to jungle. There are grasses to plant among the ferns or at the edge of the woods, in a wild-flower rock garden, or naturalized in a meadow.

Stop and think about the variety of flower and foliage among the native grasses—not to mention their uses in winter and in dried bouquets and the fact that the grass family also provides rice, wheat, oats, corn, bamboo, barley, rye, sorghum, and sugar. Suddenly you realize that the wild garden can only benefit from their presence. And I haven't mentioned the number of birds that will flock to your backyard to polish off the various seeds.

That doesn't mean that wild grasses can't be mixed with the civilized plants—they can. But to balance the rare and delicate hues of our native wildflowers, nothing quite beats the rhythmic pattern of the wild grasses.

Bottlebrush grass *(Hystrix patula)* is perfectly named. The botanical name derives from *hystrix,* the Greek name for porcupine, and *patula,* meaning "spreading." Its common alias is equally apt. Bottlebrush grass is one of the few grasses at home either in sun or in shade, but it likes damp soil. The plant is often found growing along streams at the borders of deep woods. Try a clump of these grasses planted within a cluster of sumac trees. The blossoms reach a height of four feet. Agnes Chase, a noted American agrostologist, wrote of this plant,

> On an open wooded slope a colony of Hystrix with its slender gray stems, spreading leaves, and swaying heads of horizontally spreading long-awned spikelets, suggests a dance of the nymphs.

If you can't find a source for plants, check the seed exchanges or look for it along back roads, growing on slopes and near ditches. The seed is ripe by the end of summer and easily germinated.

Broadleaf uniola, or northern sea oats *(Chasmanthium latifolium),* is probably the most beautiful of the native grasses. The botanical name, from *chasme,* "gaping," and *anthe,* "flower," refers to the open form of the blossoms. Even before they appear, the garden form is neat and attractive. The open panicles start out green and eventually turn brown. They will remain whatever color they are when picked, making them especially valuable for flower arrangers.

Originally a native of the eastern woods, broadleaf uniola can still, on rare occasions, be found in the wild. But it is also carried by most nurseries, so buy it there. If started from seed, plants will usually not bloom until the second year. The plants in bloom reach a height of about four feet and do quite well in partial shade, especially in the South.

Try a number of plants set in the midst of shrubbery or at the edge of a rhododendron thicket.

Cord grass *(Spartina pectinata)* gets its genus name from the Greek *spartine,* a rope made from *spartes,* a species of broom. The word was probably applied to this grass because of its tough leaves. The common names include bull grass, tall marsh grass, slough grass *(slough* is an Anglo-Saxon word meaning "wet or marshy place"), freshwater cord grass, and upland creek grass. American pioneers used it to thatch roofs and protect haystacks against the weather. The variegated form usually offered by nurseries has tough leaves edged with a thin band of butterscotch-yellow.

Try this grass at the edge of a clearing so that the hairlike quality of the leaf blades shows up against a dark background. Bulbs can be interplanted for spring bloom, their ripening leaves then disappearing as the cord grass grows.

If I had to name ten plants for any wild garden, Fraser's sedge *(Carex fraseri)* would definitely be one of my choices. It is not a true grass. The evergreen, straplike leaves resemble those of a lily, and instead of typical grass flowers, it bears two-foot spikes of white flowers like little mops, which appear in early spring. The genus is from *keiro*, "to cut," referring to the minutely toothed edges on some of the leaves and their ability to cut.

The soil must be rich in humus and have plenty of moisture and shade except when the leaves have yet to appear in spring. Unless given adequate protection, this sedge is only hardy from USDA Zone 6 and south.

Gray's sedge *(Carex grayi)* is another carex that forms a handsome clump of light green, grasslike leaves with a papery texture. Though adaptable to most soils and locations, it does prefer moist soil and at least partial sun. The flowers appear in mid to late summer and, although blooming along two-foot stems, are easily overlooked. But the resulting fruiting bodies look for all the world like the glass and wrought-iron hanging lights found in hallways and entrance porticos of Spanish stucco houses of the 1920s.

Indian grass *(Sorghastrum avenaceum)* looks so much like a civilized form of sorghum that it's easy to see why the botanical name is taken from the name of true *Sorghum* coupled with the Latin suffix *-astrum,* meaning "a poor imitation of."

This is a bold but graceful grass. The American answer to the Japanese eulalia grass *(Miscanthus* spp.), not only for grace but for the color of the blossoms. Reaching a height of four to five feet, the foliage would be welcome in its own right, but add long, upright, arching golden bronze panicles that appear in early September and last about a month, and you have a potential star on your hands. Place the plants at the back of a wild garden or border so that smaller plants provide interest during the summer months.

Indian rice grass *(Oryzopsis hymenoides)* comes from the Southwest, grows one to two feet tall, wants sandy soil, and is extremely drought resistant. The botanical name is from *oruza,* "rice," for its supposed resemblance to the cereal rice. The

American Indians collected the seeds and ground them for flour.

A clump of this grass calls for a piece of Pueblo pottery nearby. The seeds make a beige cloud that seems to float just above the ground. It is beautiful not only in the wild garden but also along the edge of a meadow. Just make sure it gets full sun and the soil is perfectly drained.

Blue gramma grass *(Bouteloua gracilis)* and side-oats gramma *(B. curtipendula)* are two more gifts from the Southwest. They are named for the Boutelou brothers, Claudio and Esteban, but I haven't the foggiest idea what either of them did to merit the honor. Blue gramma is an excellent lawn grass to replace what people traditionally used in arid climates. But its best feature is the blossoms that resemble caterpillars on the horizontal, clasping the stems at one end and pointing to the sky with the other. They also look like disembodied eyebrows.

Side-oats gramma's greatest charm is in the flowers that look like little oats up and down the stem with the male stamens revealing a truly bright orange as the blossoms open. Both grasses look great with stone and are perfect for rocky meadows.

Switch grass *(Panicum virgatum)* is one of the most valuable native grasses of the prairies. The botanical name comes from the Latin word for the common millet. This grass is another natural for a wild garden; it's best suited for mass planting at the edge of a field. When used as a screen to block out an unwanted subject, it gives an excellent effect. The open panicles are the most attractive when viewed against a dark background. Switch grass will withstand poor drainage and flooding, growing with wet feet in spring and dry in the summer. The roots go so deeply into the subsurface that weather changes are not serious; on the prairies it easily survived those roaring fires that once swept across the grasslands.

Wild rye *(Elymus canadensis)* has three-foot stems and, from

July to September, bears nodding heads of long curving bristles each about six inches long. The leaves are graceful and of a blue-green color with the blossoms bristly like a squirrel's tail. In nature the plants are found along riverbanks and especially in sandy soil.

COLLINSON'S HERB FOR HORSES

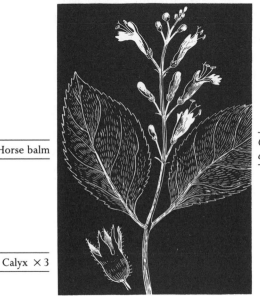

Horse balm

Collinsonia canadensis

Calyx × 3

Every so often a plant or flower is relegated to a obscure position in the garden scene because of lack of publicity, a poor name, bad press in general, or all of the above. *Collinsonia canadensis* – horse balm, horseweed, citronella, richweed, or stoneroot – is such a plant. This herb is named in honor of Peter Collinson, a London Quaker and linen-draper who became a botanist after he fell in love with gardening.

Collinson led a marvelous life at a time when degrees and connections weren't always necessary to get ahead in research and development. Over the years, he was a correspondent of the great Linnaeus and of John Bartram, another Quaker, who lived near Philadelphia and with his own hands built a beautiful house and a marvelous botanic garden. Collinson gave Bartram much advice in letters, including how to study fossils and mosses, how to mount butterflies for safe transport across the Atlantic, and how to make a rhubarb tart.

Horse balm belongs to a genus of flowers found in North America that give off a lemony odor and taste. The sap contains many alkaloids including the same antioxidants or preservatives found in rosemary. Medical experts advise caution, however, since very small doses of fresh leaves can cause vomiting.

"Horse balm" does not mean a balm for horses but refers to the rather coarse growth pattern of the plant and its old-time use as a curing and soothing agent. "Stoneroot" means not that the root is unusually hard but that the root was used in a medicinal extract for the treatment of kidney and bladder stones, as reported in herbals of the past and in the seventh edition of *Potter's New Cyclopedia of Medicinal Herbs and Preparations*.

Horse balm is a member of the very large mint family and can easily be identified as such because of the stout square stem that characterizes all family members.

Much too rangy for the formal garden bed, horse balm is an excellent choice for the wild garden, the wildflower garden, or the edge of a small woods. The plant prefers a rich, moist soil at the edge of a shaded area, and the better the surroundings, the larger it grows. My plant suffers along in an upgraded red shale and clay bank but still manages to grow three feet high and produce dozens of the little yellow flowers. It is propagated by root division in the spring.

Since the lemony smell is evident for a long distance on warm and humid days, the bees find the flowers a great place to buzz about. Bumblebees and smaller bees that land on the fringed lower lip of the blossom find it too slim to hold their weight. As it droops, they instinctively grab at the two long stamens and pollen falls upon their backs where the wings are jointed. After taking nectar, the bees fly off to other flowers. If buds are newly opened, only the forked stigma protrudes, since the stamens are still folded up. The bees then brush the stigmas without taking new pollen. Cross-pollination is thus ensured. In fact, after the stamens unfold and emerge from the blossom, the stigma's fork turns away to prevent self-fertilization.

The intricacies of horse balm pollination were first described by William Hamilton Gibson (1850–1896)—not to be confused with Charles Dana Gibson of the famous Gibson Girl. An American artist of great note, William Gibson illustrated for the *American Agriculturist* and wrote many books, including *Camp Life in the Woods* (1882) and *Our Edible Toadstools and Mushrooms* (1895).

THE GARDENER DID IT

Wild monkshood

Aconitum uncinatum

I've been reading English mysteries for years. When it comes to ingenious plot devices, inventive methods of dispatch, and adroit detectives to ferret out the clues, plus old manor houses with thunderstorms raging outside and emotions doing the same within, nothing beats them.

One of the more interesting methods of murder in English books has been poisoning. Arsenic is popular, especially in the guise of rat poison. But for every tin of evil purchased at the chemist's, a teaspoon of something leading to a noxious end has been found in the garden. And among the poisonous plants that have been quietly blooming in the perennial border, the apothecary's garden, and the monastic knot of herbs, none has a more interesting or deadly history than the monkshood, or aconite.

Also known as friar's cap, helmet flower, soldier's cap, and wolfsbane, this interesting rather than beautiful flower became part of a modern myth when it was named by the old Gypsy woman (played by Maria Ouspenskaya, for all those film buffs among us) in the 1941 horror epic *The Wolf Man:*

> *Even a man who is pure at heart*
> *And says his prayers by night,*
> *Can become a wolf when the wolfbane blooms*
> *And the autumn moon is bright.*

The botanical name is *Aconitum,* from a word used by Theophrastus for a posionous plant. The species usually cultivated in the garden is *napellus* or *henryi,* but other species and cultivars are now appearing on the market. The poison contained within the plant is aconitine, and it can be quite deadly.

There are many species of monkshood. All are native to the north temperate zone, including the trailing wolfsbane *(Aconitum reclinatum)* of the southern Allegheny Mountains, which bears white flowers, and the wild monkshood *(A. uncinatum),* which blooms from Maryland to South Carolina with flowers of deep blue.

Back in the twelfth century, monkshood was often grown as an ingredient in a poultice used for the treatment of creaking joints. The ground root of monkshood was mixed with mustard oil and flax seed oil, then rubbed into the aching joint, where it created a tingling and warm sensation. As a weapon, monkshood has been featured in the medieval thriller *Monkshood* (1981) by Ellis Peters, in which the poultice is dropped into the sauce of a roasted partridge eaten by one Gervase Bonel, who dies within an hour.

In *Death's Bright Dart* (1967), by V. C. Clinton Baddely, the elderly Cambridge don-turned-detective Dr. R. V. Davie deals with college murder involving aconitine, once again taken from the garden. Another thriller, *The Murder of My Aunt,* by Richard Hull (1934), tells of sullen and selfish nephew Edward, who takes monkshood roots from his aunt's perennial border, grinds them up, and does her in. This "ingenious plot [is] marred for us by a streak of cruelty beyond the needs of modernism in crime," commented Jacques Barzun and Wendell Hertig Taylor in *A Catalogue of Crime* (1971).

Plants bloom in late summer and fall. The violet or blue flowers are about one and a half inches high on stems to three feet. The palmately lobed leaves are two to four inches wide. All parts of the plant are poisonous, especially roots and seeds, and some cases of inadvertent poisoning have resulted from mistaking the roots for horseradish.

According to the *AMA Handbook of Poisonous and Injurious Plants,* aconitine and the related alkaloids cause an immediate tingling, burning sensation of the lips, tongue, mouth, and throat. Numbness and a feeling of constriction in the throat follow, making speech difficult. The victim suffers blurry vision and his world turns yellow-green. That, however, is not what kills him. Death results from cardiac arrhythmia.

Monkshood will flourish in ordinary soil that is fairly moist. It is especially suitable for shady or semishady positions and is best grown in groups of three or more. Plant them in spring, and when they have become well established, they will form large clumps. Roots resent disturbance.

Although monkshood is a strangely beautiful plant, I would suggest care when planting it in the wild garden—or at least leaving it unlabeled—if there's a nephew in the family who really wants to get ahead.

PURE GOLD

Sweet goldenrod — Solidago odora

It's been years since I attended a high school football game and cheered the home team to victory. But I still remember those fine autumn days with sweatered classmates sharing hard bleachers under a shiny, cloud-flecked sky.

The colors of our school were blue and gold. It's a combination that comes to mind every September as the afternoons shorten and the nights chill, with fall just down the line of days and the fields awash with goldenrods, sparked here and there with the blues of the autumn asters.

The goldenrods suffer a bad press. TV weather forecasters invariably run pictures of these tall wands of tiny flowers and accuse them of contributing to viewer's hay fever problems.

That, of course, is nonsense. The pollen of these plants is too heavy to fly easily through the air. The nasal problems of allergy sufferers is traced instead to ragweed, *Ambrosia* spp., a nondescript plant hidden beneath the noble goldenrods. Its tiny, bell-like green flowers throw their irritating pollen to the winds.

There are at last count some 130 species in the goldenrod genus *Solidago* (from the Latin *solidare,* meaning "to unite" and referring to healing properties). And each of these plants freely hybridizes with its relatives, so the final tally is beyond comprehension. Flower guides caution that identification is often difficult, but goldenrods can be grouped according to the following general types: plumelike and graceful, branched like an elm, clublike and showy, slender and wandlike, and flat-topped.

Among the more common varieties are the tall goldenrod, *Solidago altissima,* a burst of bright yellow, plumelike flowers that grows to six feet; the Canadian goldenrod, *S. canadensis,* an elm-branched type up to five feet; and the sweet goldenrod, *S. odora,* another plumelike plant with leaves that smell of anise when crushed. The gray goldenrod, *S. nemoralis,* is wandlike and gets its common name not from the flower color but from the grayish stem, which is densely coated with fine hairs. This last species is often found on dry banks along the edge of a woods.

Some years ago a clump of *Solidago altissima* appeared where the field meets the area we cut for lawn (a euphemism here for shortened grass). I trimmed the field grasses around it, then exposed a ring of dirt around the plant itself. As I worked in some composted cow manure, I could almost feel the roots moving beneath my feet. By the next season the clump was over my head and made a stunning specimen plant to relieve the green of that stubbled lawn.

The problem with goldenrods is the curse of being common. If there were only one plant per acre, they would have been pushed to extinction years ago by gardeners wishing to have them in their perennial borders – for Americans are well known for ignoring the beauty in their own woods and fields and being overly impressed by plants from other nations. But the English, a nation of true gardeners, have taken many of the common goldenrod species and, through plant hybridization, produced a number of beautiful named cultivars. Look for 'Cloth of Gold', bearing golden flowers on eighteen-inch stems, and 'Crown of Rays', with yellow flowers; both bloom in late summer. And for those of you with small gardens or even rock gardens, there are now miniature types: 'Gold Dwarf' barely reaches a foot in height, and 'Minuta' is a perfect candidate for the rock garden since it never attains even three inches in the border.

But don't overlook the fields. If you spy an especially attractive plant, ask permission to remove it and add it to your home garden. Because of the endless cross-hybridizations of nature, you never know when you might find the plant of the decade.

BOTTLE BLUE

Bottle gentian

Gentiana andrewsii

On an autumn day, I can't resist a walk in the woods: What better thing to do when the sky is a crystal blue with not a touch of cloud and the fields are full of goldenrod waving in the wind?

Deep in the woods all the ferns have turned a rich golden brown, for even though the frost has yet to reach them in those protected places, their shopworn leaves give the impression that they know the year is winding down.

Here and there are the asters of autumn. The white wood aster *(Aster divaricatus)* has a two-foot high zigzag stem and heart-shaped leaves on a short stalk. Nearby, in full bloom, is *A. acuminatus,* the whorled white wood aster–so called not because of the flowers but because the leaves are scattered up and down the stem in such a way as to appear whorled. Both asters sparkle in their shaded settings.

There's a spot in our wild garden where the sumac grove has become fairly thick. Here hay-scented ferns grow in combination with some oak seedlings (I cut them back for a short-term hedge), making a shadowed dell. It's a perfect backdrop for some clumps of these white-flowered asters, their blossoms being especially beautiful in early morning or at dusk.

It's not unusual to find a honeybee or two clutching to an aster and waiting for the sun to warm up that corner of the woods enough so they can find their way back to the hive.

But as I walk, I see out of the corner of my eye that deep and lovely blue that can only belong to the bottle gentian. Also called the closed or blind gentian *(Gentiana andrewsii),* this plant blooms from mid-September to October, usually in slightly acid and moist soil and always in a spot that offers partial shade.

The genus is named for King Gentius of Illyrica, who is credited with discovering the medicinal value of gentian root. But the plant that was once used in folk medicine was the stiff gentian, or ague-weed *(Gentiana quinquefolia),* its root being used to prepare a bitter tonic to stimulate digestion or treat headaches.

Regardless of remedies for digestion, that deep and intense blue is reason enough to grow most of the flowers in this genus—a colony of gentians is a thrill to the eye. But how this particular species is pollinated even though it never opens makes it a fitting lesson in natural history.

The agent is not the usual insect; this is a flower not designed for the immigrant honeybee. No, the insect here is the native bumblebee. Only she is heavy enough to push her way into the cavern by thrusting her tongue between the five overlapping lobes of the blossom.

She will land in the midst of a flower cluster and with great care select the younger flowers; they are marked with a bit of white that shines against the rest of the flower's gentian blue. The old flowers that have lost most of their nectar to earlier visits turn a deep reddish purple, and the white markings fade away.

If you have a few moments, watch the bumble work away as she throws her entire body weight into the push, becoming the solid sesame that will open this particular door. Once inside, only her hind legs and the tip of her abdomen stick out into the chilly air.

After a great deal of noise (she constantly mumbles to herself while at work), she will back out of the flower, make a cursory attempt at brushing the golden dust from her head and into her pollen baskets, and quickly – for a bumblebee – buzz off to another fresh flower.

In the wild garden the bottle gentian wants slightly acid soil and partial shade, and soil that has plenty of humus and never dries out. In our woods the soil is but an inch or so of leafy litter and some good black dirt, then rocks. But this is all to a gentian root's liking: Because of the continual change in temperature and the condensation of moisture from the woodsy atmosphere, a little water always coats the rocks.

FLOWERS THAT NEVER FADE

Pearly everlasting

*Anaphalis
margaritacea*

The autumn is often a melancholy time of the year, since it leads from the sunny, late summer days of September into the gray skies and dark afternoons of November – and in the mountains, to the first sticking snow. But in those years when the jet stream is favorable and Canadian highs settle over the mountains of the Northeast, we get an Indian summer, a time of crystal blue skies and a friendly sun that warms the frost-burned fields and suffuses the leaves with a golden glow. And then the garden is a beautiful place to be. As Robert Frost wrote,

I end not far from my going forth
By picking the faded blue
Of the last remaining aster flower
To carry again to you.

If last summer you had been fortunate enough to plant a clump of an attractive wildflower called pearly everlasting, there would be more than asters to carry home. That flower would now be evident as a white bouquet shining in the midst of your garden, unharmed by rains or frost and waiting for the coming mantle of snow. For the petals of everlasting have the ability to dry like tough paper and remain pure and durable.

There are two schools of thought on this everlasting quality. Neltje Blanchan wrote,

> An imaginary blossom that never fades has been the dream of poets from Milton's day; but seeing one, who loves it? Our [flower] has the aspect of an artificial [bloom]–stiff, dry, soulless, quite in keeping with the decorations on the average farmhouse mantelpiece–a wreath about flowers made from the lifeless hair of some dear departed.

James Edward Smith expressed a more positive opinion of pearly everlasting in his book of English botany:

> This flower, from its purity and durability, is an elegant emblem of immortality and is a common favorite in cottage gardens . . . where it is most beautiful.

So as with most things in the world, there are two schools of thought.

I still like the flower, not only in the garden but in those dried arrangements for the winter table. The petals are really modified leaves; the true flowers are the tiny yellow or brown florets in the center of each blossom. The stems are covered with a cottony substance meant to prevent wandering ants from stealing the nectar intended for small bees and flies.

This wildflower belongs to the genus *Anaphalis* (a Greek name for another everlasting flower). The familiar flower of the American field is *A. margaritacea*. The species name is, I think, a reference to the Marguerite daisy. A more genteel type from the Himalaya is shorter in stature and called *A. triplinervis*. Clumps are easily divided and moved, but it's best to do this in early spring. The attractive gray-green leaf color of both species looks good in the summer garden long before the blossoms appear. Give the plants a spot in full sun. Any reasonable soil will do.

Flower heads were once used as the ingredients of expectorants in treating colds, but this seems to have been out of favor for the last eighty or so years.

STARS OF THE FIELDS

New England aster

Aster novae-angliae

The asters are a pretty lot—at least by day. Unlike the stars for which they are named, these blossoms go in at night.

If you closely examine some of the asters blooming along the rural roadside, you see many variations: What at first seems lavender turns out to be shades of rose, and there are light and dark blues and pinks, and some blossoms that are almost white. If you move the wild sorts into the garden, they will usually get bigger and, unless staked, eventually flop over. But in future seasons you can cut the wildings back in early to midsummer and thus control future growth.

Asters belong to the daisy or Compositae family. The true flowers are tubes in the golden centers full of nectar and dusted with pollen; the so-called petals are really the ray flowers, there to attract the insect with their lovely colors. They hybridize with ease, and the chance of finding a shade of color that departs from the species is fairly good because there are hundreds of crosses.

Native American species include the deep violet New York aster, *Aster novae-belgii*, found along the eastern coast from Newfoundland to Georgia; the very showy, deeper violet of the New England aster, *A. novae-angliae*, a ubiquitous species that grows from Vermont to Alabama, west to North Dakota, Wyoming, and New Mexico (the American Indians used this plant as a root tea for treating fever and diarrhea); and the upland white aster, *A. ptarmicoides*, which likewise grows throughout the country. This last aster is the first to bloom of the white asters, starting in late July.

Most of the garden cultivars of the late-blooming asters are the result of hybrids usually derived from both the New England and the New York asters plus the input of the Italian aster, *Aster amellus*.

These plants need only full sun and plenty of water; they are tolerant of most soils. The following cultivars all begin to bloom in September and continue well into October. *Aster* 'Alma Potschke'–a cultivar of mixed parentage, but any plant with a name like that must be good–has salmon-tinged rose flowers on three-foot stems. 'Harrington's Pink' has pure pink flowers on three- to four-foot stems. And 'September Beauty' bears flowers of deep crimson on forty-inch stems.

One year, in preparation for an autumn garden, I went out in the fields looking for the brightest pink and the deepest blue asters I could find. I marked the plants with colored tape and dug them up the following spring, trimming them back severely. They were set on a gentle rocky slope that eventually edged up to the woods. To give them a good start, I mixed in some composted sheep manure (cow dung works just as well) and loosened the rock and shale that sat just beneath a thin layer of topsoil. That autumn, people asked what nursery they came from.

The following asters are all American natives. *Aster cordifolius,* the blue wood aster, is perfect in light shade. The heath aster *(A. ericoides)* has produced a cultivar 'Golden Spray', a twenty-four-inch plant with golden flowers and attractive foliage. *A. lateriflorus,* usually about four feet high, is represented in the trade by 'Horizontalis', whose tiny panicles of lilac flowers bloom above horizontal branches of leaves that turn coppery purple for fall. This last plant is unusual since the species is an American wildflower called the calico or starved aster (the second description due to the visible stems) introduced into English gardens in 1829. It certainly takes a long time for an American beauty to return home to fame and fortune.

THE PATRON SAINT
OF GARDENERS

St. Fiacre

Most noble endeavors of mankind have a patron saint, usually a man or woman who has achieved notoriety—often by suffering torture or death—in that particular field. In A.D. 303, for example, a woman named Barbara, who dwelt in Heliopolis (a city a few miles below Cairo), was decapitated by her father when she refused to renounce Christianity—whereupon he was consumed by lightning, and she became the patron saint of firearms (but not the N.R.A.) and all accidents from explosions involving gunpowder.

In A.D. 250, Apollonia became the patron saint of dentistry. Because she would not relinquish her faith, all her teeth were brutally removed, one by one, with a pair of pincers, and she was then burned alive. Most patron saints had such ends.

One late summer day I went to a garden party and saw a sculpture of an Irish monk named St. Fiacre. The plaque below called him the patron saint of gardening. In my quarter-century of walking through gardens and garden centers, I have encountered statue after statue of a pious man in a cloak, identified by crude signs as St. Francis, but never an Irish monk named Fiacre.

Apparently today's concrete casters believe that the saint devoted to the art of gardening would talk to the birds and think quiet thoughts. I always dismissed St. Francis out of hand since tradition, I reasoned, would probably demand that any patron saint of gardening be buried alive while hoeing beans, gored by a team of oxen while tilling bottomland, or forced to endure plagues of locusts and mealybugs.

And it turns out I was right. St. Fiacre was not a quiet man of God but a wildman of gardening, a miracle worker who bargained with the church, had problems with a witch, and is the patron saint not only of gardeners but of cabdrivers as well.

My *Webster's Second International Dictionary* (the only true dictionary) was of no help in my detective work; it gives *fiacre* as the name of a taxicab in France. Next I consulted *The Compact Edition of the Oxford English Dictionary* and found reference once again to the cab and a passing notice of St. Fiacre's being the name of a Paris hotel.

Albert Forbes Sieveking's *Gardens Ancient and Modern*, published in 1899, did mention St. Fiacre as the patron saint of gardeners and, on page 115, mentions that the Confrère de Saint Fiacre, the tutelar saint of horticulturists, were still holding their gardener's lodge meetings at the King's Fruit and Kitchen Garden at Versailles, just before 1700.

But it was Dion Clayton Calthrop's *The Charm of Gardens,* from 1910, that told the whole story of the saint.

Back in the Ireland of the 600s, in a continuing effort to spread the word of God, various monks were sent to Europe, among them Fiacre. With pilgrim's staff, reed pen, and true belief, these holy men went from country to country spreading the message of God by means of illuminated manuscripts, an art in which the Irish of that time excelled.

Fiacre soon made a name for himself as a pious monk but wished to become a hermit. So the Bishop of Paris gave him a place of his own, deep in the forest and away from the monastery, where Fiacre retired to the great work of his life. He soon cleared a space in the woods and built an oratory to Our Lady and a small hut for himself. Then he began a garden. And the garden, as is the wont of gardens and gardeners, became larger.

No record is kept of what Fiacre grew. But according to various writings of the time, such a garden would contain fruit, a lot of vegetables (meat was tough, and at a premium), and wildflowers and herbs for the medicines they contained.

Achilles Tatius, a fourth-century Greek author of pornography who was "Englished from Greeke" by Anthony Hodges in 1638, described gardens of the time as containing many trees

> whose boughes flourisht, and mutually embrac'd each other, growing so thicke, that their leaves and fruit were promiscuously mingled; upon the bigger trees grew ivie, some of it on the soft plane trees, other some sticking to the pitch tree made it tendered by its embracements . . .

According to Alexander Neckam (1157–1217), "There you should have parsely, cost, fennel, southern-wood, coriander, sage, savery, hyssop, mint, rue, ditanny, smallage, and peonies." He lists many more wildflowers, herbs, and roots, including groundsel *(Senecio* spp.), wormwood, calendulas, and three kinds of milk-vetch *(Astragalus* spp.). So we may speculate that Fiacre's garden in the woods had both a cultivated and a wild part.

Soon roaming hunters chanced upon the garden and were welcomed with open arms. They marveled to find such a place of plenty deep in the gloomy woods and heard Fiacre preach and saw witnessed his healing powers.

News spread far and wide. Fiacre had to build another hut for the visitors who came for consultations, and, of course, he ran out of land. So off he went to the bishop and asked for more.

The bishop said, "Fiacre, I will give you as much land as you can enclose with your spade in one day."

Back to his garden went Fiacre, and taking some sticks, he surveyed the amount of land he needed and marked its boundaries, an amount far in excess of what one man could hope to enclose with simple shovel in one day. Then he went into the oratory and prayed for help.

Now it so happened that an envious woman lived nearby. She was probably the previous tender of the herbs and had, until Fiacre moved in, advised all the peasants on how to treat their ailments and conduct their love lives. She saw everyone going to the monk for aid and advice, and upon hearing through the grapevine that he was up to something, hid in some bushes and watched the whole affair.

The next morning, when the monk's prayer was answered and all the land he had marked was now encircled by spadework, she went straight to the bishop and accused Fiacre of magic. But the bishop called it a miracle, made Fiacre a saint, and was so angered by the accusation of the witch that he denied the oratory to all women for all time.

Where the saint had begun his solitary garden, a great Benedictine priory was built, and many wonders of healing were credited to his saintly relics. Then sometime in the 1600s, probably as a result of urban sprawl and population pressures, his remains were moved to the cathedral at Meaux. There in 1641, Anne of Austria visited the shrine. She did not enter but remained outside the grating because legend said that any woman who went inside would go blind or mad (but not both).

With the passing of the years, the misogyny of Fiacre has apparently been overlooked. Otherwise many women gardeners would be up in arms asking that the job be given to Anne of Austria for her dalliances in the garden with the Three Musketeers or to Lucrezia Borgia for her knowledge of herbal poisons.

Now where do taxicabs come in? It seems that in 1648 a gentleman by the name of Sauvage started an establishment that rented carriages. For the business, he bought a house in the Rue St. Martin called the Hôtel de St. Fiacre. The hotel had a figure of the saint over the doorway. The coach in question was a small four-wheeled carriage, hung with double springs, and soon all the coaches of Paris were called *fiacres*. The drivers placed images of the saint on their dashboards and named him their patron. The English called fiacres "miserable vehicles," and although Charles Dickens wrote in *A Tale of Two Cities* that the victims of the French Revolution were taken to the guillotine in tumbrels or carts, I like to think that aristocrats were really driven in fiacres—so before they lost their heads, their backs were in disrepair. And judging by the taxi rides I've endured over the passing years, the good St. Fiacre has had far more influence on the gardeners of the world than on the taxi drivers.

COLCHICUM AND SAFFRON

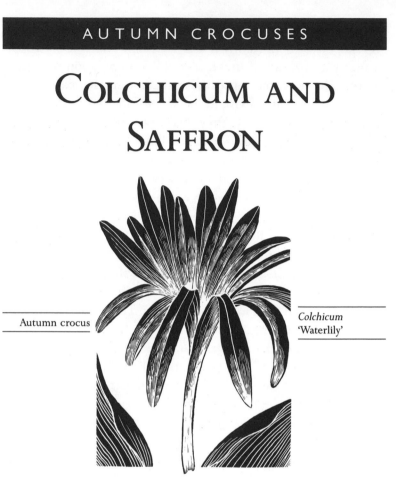

Autumn crocus

Colchicum 'Waterlily'

Whenever the gleaners come through the garden, I know that autumn is fast approaching. We call them gleaners because they spend the daylight hours paying attention to every square inch of ground, looking for seeds and other things to eat; the rest of the world calls them slate-colored juncos.

But what really brought the season to my attention was the sight of my colchicums—or as they are sometimes called, the true autumn crocus—beginning to bloom (in a bed backed by a long line of golden brown gloriosa daisies) just about a month too early.

There in the front garden my entire planting of *Colchicum byzantium* is flowering to beat the band. The rosy lilac flowers are three and a half inches across on three-inch stalks and full of bees from dawn to dusk. It certainly does not bode well for a late winter if these blossoms are any clue to upcoming climatic events.

Now, colchicum is a drug plant from antiquity and has a long history in the annals of pharmacy. It's first mentioned in the Ebers Papyrus, the world's oldest medical text, an Egyptian document prepared about 1550 B.C.

In ancient Greece, the root and plant gatherers were well acquainted with the medicinal properties of colchicum. The genus is named for the land of Colchis at the eastern tip of the Black Sea, a mysterious place steeped in myth and legend; it's the spot where Jason encountered Medea and found the Golden Fleece.

No rodent ever bothers these corms; the vermin sense that the cellular contents are not all that great for their digestive systems. As a poison, the alkaloid colchicine has been featured in a number of mystery stories. Edmund Crispen, in his novel *Frequent Hearses,* confounds his detective until the last demise by having the murderer place a lethal dose of this ancient potion in another character's medicine after distilling the poison from a number of corms of *C. autumnale,* the species with the highest content of the drug.

The action of the pure, crystalline chemical upon the cell division and growth processes of plants is well known, and the drug has opened new vistas in experimental agriculture. Used properly, colchicine has a strange paralyzing effect on a plant's chromosomes, those parts of the cell that determine the plant's character. It causes a divided cell to have more than its normal number of chromosomes. This condition, called polyploidy, can result in startling effects: Giant flowers, taller stems, increased vigor, and greater hardiness are among those noticed in botanical laboratories.

When this property was first discovered – in the 1920s – hybridizers rushed out to purchase the drug for use in treating seedlings. It's still used for this purpose today. In fact, the gloriosa daisies blooming behind my autumn crocuses owe their spectacular display to colchicine and the work of Dr. Albert F. Blakeslee. In 1919 he began collecting plants of the native black-eyed Susan, then selecting the most promising for further study. He began hybridizing with the aim of increasing plant vigor and the flower size and color range. Then after selecting and reselecting for many years, he treated the best with colchicine to produce tetraploid flowers of maximum size. *Rudbeckia hirta* 'Gloriosa' is the result.

So there they both are, flowering in the fall border: one plant that has remained the same for thousands of years, and one changed beyond recognition because of a chemical derived from the first.

Colchicums are best naturalized. The flowers appear without leaves in the fall and the leaves themselves show up in spring. They are not dainty but rather coarse – even though pleasantly pleated – and they turn from green to yellow to brown as the spring sun creeps to the zenith. These are admirable colors in November but not in June. So the best place for autumn crocus is under deciduous trees or at the edge of wild gardens or in a part of the lawn that you can let alone until the leaves die back. In a number of semiwild places about the garden we've set out several autumn crocus species. Their glorious mauve-tinted double flowers pop up in stark contrast to the browns of the crumpled leaves blown about by the winds.

One of the loveliest is a hybrid cultivar, *Colchicum* 'Water-lily'. These flowers are talked about in all the bulb catalogs as though they were something new. But in reality they were created—according to *Index Hortensis*—before 1927 by one Zocher & Co. I know nothing about that company, but none of the colchicum variations developed since can hold a candle to this one. Ours were planted on September 15 and began to bloom in mid-October. Soil must be well drained, and since the six-inch leaves do not appear until the following spring, care must be taken in placement of the corms.

Another favorite is *Colchicum autumnale,* called mysteria, naked ladies, the wonder bulb, and meadow saffron—though it has nothing to do with true saffron, which is a crocus. The flowers bloom from late September to October; they are between three and four inches high, and the leaves are up to a foot long.

Many species of colchicum are available today. But gardeners have to be careful about the sources. For these are originally wildflowers—or, I guess, wild bulbs—and many nurseries buy bulbs taken from the wild rather than spend time in propagation.

Now, fall-flower crocuses (not to be confused with the colchicums) are members of the iris family. Like their spring-blooming relatives, they are welcome in the garden scene, especially on bright sunny days when they open all their petals wide. They bloom from early September to November. The genus is an ancient name used by Theophrastus.

Plant the corms four inches deep and three inches apart, always in well-drained soil and full sun or only under deciduous trees. After three or four years you will note that the corms have risen to—if not above—the surface of the ground. This is because new corms form on top of the old, just like bricks added to a wall, and eventually reach the surface. When this happens, just dry them off and replant in July. And remember, as with other bulbs the leaves must die back naturally in order for the corms to store enough food for the next year's flowering.

Usually the leaves follow the flowers, but sometimes they do not appear until the following spring.

Crocus asturicus bears violet-purple flowers about four inches long in mid-October. The stamens are a bright orange. Twelve-inch leaves appear during and after blooming. Louise Beebe Wilder, writing in *Hardy Bulbs,* calls this the Spanish crocus and reports that in its native mountains it's called *Espanto Pastores,* or "Terror of Shepherds," since it appears just after the autumn rains and presages the coming of winter. It is hardy from Zone 6 south.

Crocus sativus is the saffron crocus, which has been cultivated as a spice and coloring agent since the time of the ancient Hebrews. The flowers are a rich purple; they grow four inches high and appear from October to November. If you are interested in going into the business of gathering saffron, you might be surprised to know that it takes thirty-five thousand flowers to yield eight ounces of the stuff. Sometimes saffron crocus survives in colder climates when given a heavy mulch, but it's usually best to grow them in Zone 6 or above.

Crocus speciosus is the earliest of the fall bloomers, usually appearing in mid to late September. The flowers are clear blue on two- or three-inch stems. It's the only autumn crocus that was ever reliably hardy in our northern garden. 'Albus' has white flowers, 'Globosus' blue, and the variety *Pollux* bears the largest flowers of the species, up to three inches across.

THE PASSENGER PIGEON BERRY

Pokeweed

Phytolacca americana

The pokeweed is an American original viewed as a weed by most gardeners in the States but prized as a garden plant by the English. It is also known as the scoke, ink berry, garget, and pigeon-berry (so called in honor of the now extinct passenger pigeon, birds that relished the berries).

Often when walking through the more sophisticated English gardens in the late fall, you will see this plant at the back of the border. William Robinson, in his book *The English Flower Garden* (1900), described it as a North American perennial . . . scarcely refined enough in leaf for the flower garden, but effective near the rougher approaches of a hardy fernery, in open glades near woodland walks, or in any like position.

Known as *Phytolacca decandra,* it has white flowers with green (more like chartreuse) centers, pink-tinted outside, about a quarter-inch across, on bending arches up to eight inches long. Whether in bloom or on its way to becoming lustrous black berries, the plant is a showstopper.

In a spot to its liking, pokeweed can attain a height of more than eight feet, becoming a large, open bush with stems that flush with red toward the end of the summer. Thoreau described the plant as "all on fire with ripeness" and used the stout, vigorous stem for a cane.

A number of bird species will flock to the berries. As a result, seed is found in a great many places—in fact, wherever flickers, robins, woodpeckers, and rose-breasted grosbeaks gather.

Often in the fall, children of the city folk, attracted to the flagrant color of the plant, eat the shiny berries—to a bad effect. The berries can upset the stomach. The leaves and the roots are poisonous, too. But in some parts of the country the young shoots are cooked and eaten like asparagus. The American Indians and early American settlers used the root as an emetic and cathartic. The convoluted rootstock resembles mandrake and each year sends up the stout, branching stems that flower in midsummer.

According to statistics gathered by various poison control centers across the United States, pokeweed is second on the list of plant species most frequently involved in accidental ingestion.

According to the *AMA Handbook of Poisonous and Injurious*

Plants, the mature berries are relatively nontoxic. Troubles arise from eating uncooked leaves in salads or from eating roots, sometimes mistaken for parsnips.

The toxin, phytolaccatoxin and related triterpenes, goes to work within two or three hours after ingestion, causing nausea and gastroenteric cramps, profuse sweating, and persistent vomiting later accompanied by diarrhea. The effects may last forty-eight hours.

Although dangerous, pokeweed is worth having in the wild garden where, if treated with care, it can become a plant of distinction. And if you are worried, remember that we grow rhubarb with abandon. Yet this old garden favorite can cause great distress (and worse) if the raw or canned leaves are eaten in any great quantity.

FOOD FOR THE BIRDS

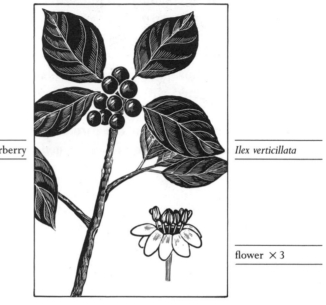

Winterberry

Ilex verticillata

flower × 3

The day after Thanksgiving was a most beautiful day: Hoarfrost sparkled with a billion glintings on every trunk, branch, and wizened leaf along the country roadways. Glowing with a brilliant red against the backdrop of silver were the carmine berries of *Ilex verticillata,* the winterberry. The year's crop was more bountiful than usual, a testament to the more-than-average water that fell during the spring and summer. At one end of Findler's Swamp, a grove of these bushes was strung with glowing berries, looking like the fairy lights that decorate the elevators in upscale hotels or fancy restaurants.

The other morning, a neighbor noted the abundance of

berries, wondering why they were so plentiful in the fall but by midwinter were mostly gone. Well, the answer is the birds. As other food supplies dwindle, our resident chickadees, blue jays, and such zero in on these tasty – at least for birds – tidbits.

Not only birds enjoy these berries. On November 19, 1857, Thoreau wrote,

> I see where a mouse which has a hole under a stump has eaten out clean the insides of the little *Prinos verticillatus* berries. . . . What pretty fruit for the mice, these bright prinos berries! They run up the twigs in the night and gather this shining fruit, take out the small seeds, and eat their kernals at the entrance to their burrows. The ground is strewn with them there.

Prinos was an old name for *ilex*.

These deciduous shrubs – sometimes small trees – are members of the holly clan, bearing the botanical name of *Ilex verticillata. Ilex* is the ancient name of the holm oak, *Quercus ilex,* an evergreen oak with dark, shining, toothed leaves resembling holly; *verticillata* means "whorled" and refers to the leaves.

Winterberries grow to a height of six to twenty feet. They are quite fond of a wettish or swampy site but will surprise all collectors of plant lore by occasionally appearing on the steepest of dry hillsides. Another name is the black alder; the smooth bark is a warm, dull gray.

Most of the year, the branches are hidden by tall field grasses, by other shrubs like the sweet bush, or by larger and bushier neighbors. The flowers are small and white, blooming in late June and early July, escaping the notice of all but the most careful observer. They could never be thought of as ornamental. Not until late autumn – when most leaves have fallen, except for the ubiquitous beech and the stately pin oak–do the beautiful and brilliant red berries begin to appear. One form, known as forma *chrysocarpa,* has yellow or orange fruit.

Hollies are dioecious (having male and female flowers on separate plants), so if you're buying trees from a nursery center or moving them in from your own property, make sure you have both kinds. The staminate flowers have many anthers and cluster where the leaf stems meet. There are fewer female flowers, and each has a prominent stigma.

This is the only species of holly that is fully winter hardy in the colder parts of America. It does well in poor soil and even partial shade and is hardy from Zone 3 southward. Plant it out in spring or fall. Protect it from local deer herds until it gains a bit of stature.

Plant breeders have been at work developing a cultivar, 'Winter Red', with darker and greener foliage than the species and more fruit. Just remember that you must have a male in the area to pollinate the female flowers.

If you wish to cut a few branches for indoor holiday decorations, cover the bushes with bird netting until you start collecting in early December. Keep the branches in water or the berries will shrivel and fall off.

After the Snow Flies

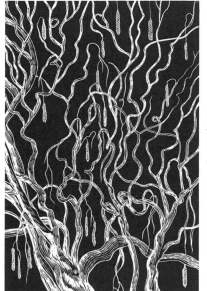

Harry Lauder's
walking stick

Corylus avellana
'Contorta'

It's easy to write about violets, asters, and daylilies when weather is warm and sun is hot, but degrees of cold are something else. When snow falls and winter storms rage, the garden writer must call forth his imagination.

On the wall over my desk is a map published by the U.S. Department of Agriculture. The map shows the ten climatic zones that ribbon across our country. Zone 5 (where the minimum winter temperatures average $-20°$ to $-10°F$) is green and extends from Newfoundland through most of New England

and New York; splits Pennsylvania, Ohio, and Illinois; takes a third of Missouri, half of Kansas and New Mexico, and one quarter of Arizona; then blots out most of Nevada, a smidgen of California, half of Oregon, and a third of Washington before shooting back up to Canada—where most gardeners say it belongs in the first place.

North of Zone 5 (except for a few areas around large bodies of water) is a gigantic area that includes four zones that are even colder down to − 50°F. South of Zone 5 only fourteen of the forty-eight contiguous states do not include at least some area rated Zone 5—even Texas has a green dot of that color in the upper northeast corner.

Starting about the end of July, gardeners in our region begin to feel the first hints of the coming cold air of winter: Early in the evening the chill slowly flows down from the mountaintops to settle eventually at the bottom of the hill. By the middle of October we've already had temperatures to 26°F.

If you live year-round in such a climate, it's not too long before the thought of the garden in winter rises to the top of your gardener's consciousness. You quickly become aware of your limitations. Soon comes the knowledge that your climate will not support flowering camellias *(Camellia japonica),* Christmas roses *(Helleborus niger),* or clumps of winter daphne *(Daphne odora)* scenting the frigid January air; the sunflowers that are still blooming will be naught but blackened stumps and all the rose hips will have been devoured by the birds.

Even the protection afforded by snowcover cannot be counted on. In our area we never get a guaranteed snowfall: In one out of five years, the snow accumulations total less than one inch. Instead we get sleet and downpours of rain. In these years, what the deer do not destroy, winter burn from the harsh and drying winds does.

The majority of plants usually suggested by English books for the winter garden are happy only when temperatures stay above 0°F. And even the gardening books written in America usually address the more civilized climatic regions. Except for a stalwart but sophisticated few, I have chosen hardier plants so that my winter garden is entirely safe where temperatures plunge and icicles proliferate.

Today, however, is unseasonably warm. Let's take advantage of this January thaw to stroll through our garden.

First we pass a large multiflora rosebush that has been growing in the same spot for more than forty years. Although the blooming period in late spring is brief, we keep the bush because of the orange hips that cover the bare branches well into late January, when they are finally consumed by the birds.

Now I realize that this *Rosa multiflora* has a bad press. During the 1960s it was touted as the living fence, keeping intruders and cattle out, yet easy to install and practically care-free. Ours was planted sometime in the 1930s, and yes, it does seed about. But if the seedlings turn up in unwanted places, they are quickly removed. If the seeds sprout in the nearby field and have the energy to outstrip the goldenrods, orchard grass, and wild daylilies, then more power to them. No, it's not a sophisticated rose. But when it blooms in May, the blossoms are sweet, and it works as a specimen plant.

Behind the rose is a mass of American bittersweet, *Celastrus scandens,* chided by some gardeners for being overly rampant—and they are right. Do not plant bittersweet in the formal garden or around the backyard. And don't plant it if you hate outside work, detest pruning, and regard yearly pilgrimages to the brush pile as unsavory occupations. In other words, couch gardeners beware. But if you confine it to the wild part of the garden and keep it cut back, you will be rewarded first by the golden yellow of the autumn leaves and then by the beautiful berries, bright orange with scarlet wrappings, that cover the twining vines.

Next on my right, as we walk down the browned grass path

that extends between the borders, is a giant clump of eulalia grass, *Miscanthus sinensis.* Its twelve-foot-high stems now sport waving brown leaves topped by silver plumes of the seed heads, blooms that will persist until the following spring.

Falling over the edge of the stone scree bed are the clambering branches of the rock cotoneaster, *Cotoneaster horizontalis,* covered from base to tip with glowing red berries, a color almost ready to clash with the pink-magenta blossoms of the heath, *Erica carnea* 'King George'. Above them both are the spiraling branches of Harry Lauder's walking stick, *Corylus avellana* 'Contorta', bare now but in early spring festooned with yellow catkins that will hang like ornaments upon the stems.

Opposite the scree bed is a low stone wall that in summer marks the edge of a bed full of lamb's ear, *Stachys byzantina* (even now their woolly leaves are still in evidence). Along the bottom edge of the wall is a line of ebony spleenwort, *Asplenium platyneuron,* green and glossy, as they will remain well into winter. A Christmas rose, *Helleborus niger,* which seldom blooms but still produces marvelous foliage, shares space with the spleenwort.

Nearby is a mound of *Sedum* 'Autumn Joy'; its flower heads will stay the color of burned mahogany until spring. Behind it is a clump of the eye-catching, red-stemmed Siberian dogwood, *Cornus alba* 'Siberica', generally nondescript in the spring and summer but making up for it when the leaves fall.

At the edge of the woods, the clumps of pearly everlasting, *Anaphalis margaritacea,* its papery white blossoms waving in a quickening wind, stand out against the darkness of the gathering night. Only a few short weeks ago that same wind rustled the yellow blossoms of the witch hazel, *Hamamelis virginiana,* and a few tattered remnants are still there, hanging on for dear life.

Back near the house, stone steps go up a slight slope to an

area shaded by a very old white pine *(Pinus strobus)*. In between the crevices of those steps are bergenias *(Bergenia cordifolia)*, plants from Siberia and Mongolia. As such they are perfectly happy in temperatures of $-30°$F, but when exposed to winds at this point, their leaves turn brown and burn at the edges until they look exactly like toast points. Above $0°$F the plants are evergreen and turn a reddish bronze. They prefer partial shade in the summer and a soil that is well drained but moist, with humus or leaf mold. In such a spot they make an excellent ground cover. Every spring they flower with rose-pink waxy blossoms that look like tiny ruffle-edged bells.

Above and beyond those steps are many ornamental grasses. In winter their colors are never blatant or bold. Tones here are mellow: Shades of brown or buff mingle with warm, burnished yellow ochers highlighted with the worn silver-white of the seed plumes that wave above, welcome and beautiful against the snows, glowing when held within a sheath of ice.

The various cultivars of the eulalia grasses *(Miscanthus* spp.) grow, on the average, over seven feet in one summer season and usually show their plumes as fall approaches. When the days grow shorter and colder, growth stops. Then, with the first killing frost, the leaves turn a rich golden yellow.

That rather steep bank that rises up behind our garden consists of poor soil, with a large percentage of small rocks and red shale. We've tried many things over the years to at least give it the rudiments of civilization. We finally solved the problem by planting staggered rows of a native American, little bluestem grass *(Schizachyrium scoparium)*. This grass grows in a fountain-like fashion, though small in scale, and bears numerous small, white seed plumes on the top of deep blue stems that turn to purple-brown in the fall.

Right now many fields in our area are awash with the warm rusty tones of little bluestem, and all the tops of these grasses are glistening in the winter sun; their silvery white blossoms open in mid-October and remain until the winds of March blow them out of the picture.

When they are planted in a semicultivated area, the individual plants thrive; even fifteen plants make a wonderful show.

At the base of the bank grow the lichens and mosses. Winter has no effect on them. And curling about the grays, greens, and browns of their elfin cups is a colony of poverty grass *(Dathonia spicata).* In summer the six-inch leaves of poverty grass are at best nondescript, but by November the leaves will have curled and look like wood shavings left by a tiny carpenter. Though heavy snows bury these plants, with every thaw their color and beauty return.

Next to the birdbath sits a clump of another American native, northern sea oats *(Chasmanthium latifolium),* which turns golden brown in the winter's sun, sporting oatlike seed heads that by December will have a frosting of ice. Pick their blossoms earlier in the garden year and they will retain their color forever. But now, thanks to the killing cold, all tints of green are gone.

We have many dwarf conifers in the garden; their steely blue and green foliage will be bright against the snow. A weeping birch that in winter becomes an abstract pattern of waving lines vies for our attention with mahogany sedums. But when winter descends from leaden skies, it's the ornamental grasses that bring warmth and beauty to the garden until spring returns to the mountains.

It's getting colder now, and the weakening rays of the setting sun have made a band of orange along the horizon. Now is the time to go back inside to the fire and think about the quiet beauty of winter and the spring that's sure to come.

What's in a Name?

Great burdock · *Arctium lappa*

Botanical names blend the words of the past with those of the present in combinations that leave neologists in constant delight and most etymologists happy as clams. But when it comes to common names, even the hardiest wordsmiths are sometimes at a loss.

Take the English names for the great burdock, a plant originally from Europe and now naturalized over most of America. Geoffrey Grigson, in his book *The Englishman's Flora* (which in its next edition will probably appear as *The Englishperson's Flora)*, lists fifty-two. A few of the choicer appellations are bachelor's buttons (bachelors can't sew and would use the Velcro approach to buttoning up); butter-dock (the large leaves were used to wrap butter); clog-weed (self-explanatory); snake's rhubarb (a sly dig at the people who eat the young shoots either cooked or raw); tuzzy-muzzy (meaning disheveled and ragged); and cuckoldy-burr-busses (I'll leave that one alone).

Now imagine what happens over the years as the spirit of education melds with the god of the mall, and people not only talk less but read less and the books all succumb to the ravages of acidic paper: In another hundred years, who will know what they mean?

The botanical names are usually easier since they often rely on combining well-documented Greek or Latin words. (But even there, problems of interpretation exist: Nobody knows where *Clemone* came from, other than that Theophrastus used it in 250 B.C., or *Lonas,* the genus of a charming little yellow annual, with a name beyond anyone's ken.) In the case of the great burdock, *Arctium* is from the Greek word *arktos,* for "bear," referring to the many coarse bristles, and *lappa* is Latin for "burr."

The common name *daisy,* as applied first to the English daisy *(Bellis perennis),* is derived from the Anglo-Saxon *daeges-eage,* indicating "eye of day," since the flower head closes at night but opens again during broad daylight. The generic *Bellis* could be linked with the Latin *bellum,* "war," because for centuries this perky little plant has figured in herbals as a cure for wounds, among other ailments. But it could equally well come from the Latin *bella,* "pretty." The specific *perennis* tells of the plant's perennial habit.

Since it is considered a weed by the people who love pure and perfect lawns, the plant breeders have been at work and transformed this young beauty into a painted charmer. There are now pom-poms, doubles, and even flowers with white petals stained with red or crimson. But in this case, I remain a purist and prefer the original wildflowers as fine additions to the wild garden and keep the cultivars for the edge of a formal border.

With the persistence of folknames, *daisy* was soon used for every like member of this large family of flowers. Take the ubiquitous oxeye, or moon daisy *(Chrysanthemum leucanthemum)*, a common weed in the view of farmers and a lovely flower for happy people to gather by the armful when walking in meadows. This is another European import, and here the common names are not lost in the mists of time but merely refer to the large yellow disk.

Quick, what's the derivation of Shasta daisy?

Luther Burbank (1849–1926), America's famous horticulturist and plant breeder, wished to produce a new garden daisy. He began by crossing the European moon chrysanthemum *(Chrysanthemum maximum)* from the Pyrenees mountains with the oxeye daisy. The results were better than expected. But Burbank thought the flowers could be still larger, so he took the new plant and crossed it with the Japanese daisy *(C. nipponicum)*, and the first Shasta daisy was born, named after Shasta, California.

Like the oxeye daisy, dandelions have a tendency to appear where they are not wanted. Then, whether by hand or chemical, they are immediately removed from lawn or flower bed. If only they were rare, the handsome golden flower heads and jagged leaves would be sought after by most gardeners. James Russell Lowell wrote in his poem "To the Dandelion,"

> *How like a prodigal doth nature seem*
> *When thou, for all thy gold, so common art!*

The common denomination dandelion *(Taraxacum officinale)* is ascribed to the French *dent de lion*, "lion's tooth." Notwithstanding that some people believe this refers to the toothlike appearance of the flower head or the tap root, it almost certainly alludes to the backward-pointing, fine-edged lobes of the somewhat bitter leaf. The French term is itself drawn from the Latin *dens* and *leo,* intimating the dentate (toothed) foliage. And if you wish to grow them in the garden, choose one of the cultivars that produces larger dark green leaves both for salads and for boiled greens, or blanch the leaves for an added treat.

Another and smaller feline is remembered in the plant that we call catnip *(Nepta cataria)* or, in England, catmint. Cats adore this plant. Indeed, our own cat, Miss Jekyll, is so keen on the scent that she will deliberately bruise or nip the stems to release the perfume. Certainly an ancient belief holds that cats crave this vegetation and, whenever they smell or sample it, immediately turn very affectionate, sportive, and "full of fight." The plants were first discovered at Nepet in Tuscany, whence *Nepeta* is derived.

The scarlet pimpernel *(Anagallis arvensis)* saw duty as a wildflower long before it became the *nom de plume* of Sir Percy Blakeney, the English fop and dandy from Kent who, in Baroness Orczy's novel, rescued distressed aristocrats from the guillotine of the French Revolution.

According to an ancient fable, the pimpernel has the power to make people laugh and be cheerful, the meaning of *anagallis* in Greek; *arvensis* refers to cultivated fields, the common habitat of this plant.

As a flower, the scarlet pimpernel (it can also be white or blue) has a host of common names, including eyebright, old man's glass eye, and poor man's weatherglass. The weather references refer to the flower's opening at about eight A.M. and closing about three P.M. and also closing in wet or damp weather. Pimpernel is from the Latin *pipinella,* which came in turn from *bipinnula,* or "two-winged," from the feathery leaves of the burnet saxifraga, *Pimpinella saxifraga.*

Since the weather bowed to this flower, it has a magical reputation. In Ireland, if it were held in the hand, the holder gained second sight and would understand the language of birds and animals. Although the leaves can give susceptible people a dermatitis, when used in a tincture they are old remedies for dropsy and rheumatic afflictions.

In the garden, pimpernels are hardy annuals, perfect as walkway edgings, spread about taller plantings of iris or sundrops, or let loose in the wild garden. Start the seeds indoors six weeks before your last frost, or plant directly outdoors in early spring. They will reseed. A particularly beautiful blue is found in the cultivar 'Gentian Blue'.

During the reign of Elizabeth I, the ruffs and frills so fashionable then were stiffened by pure white starch made from cuckoo-pint roots *(Arum maculatum)*, a plant similar to our jack-in-the-pulpit. The common name refers not to the bird but instead to the Anglo-Saxon *cucu,* meaning "lively," and *pintle,* "a perpendicular pin," descriptive of the outline of the spiked blossom.

And since the same collars could get quite soiled, the foliage of soapwort or bouncing Bet *(Saponaria officinalis)* was used for cleaning. Bouncing Bet (or sometimes Betty) is a vivacious immigrant from Europe that escaped from cultivation and is now classified as a weed of the roadside and railroad beds throughout most of temperate North America. In fact, the largest bouncing Bet colony I ever saw was on a bank just below the railroad tracks in the center of Callicoon, New York. Betty must have been a beauty to be memorialized by these blossoms.

When boiled or bruised in water, the leaves turn saponaceous, and the lather so created has all the effects of soap (it promptly cleans off grease) and was formerly used for this purpose. The Latin *sapo* means "soap." *Wort* was once favored as a synonym for *plant,* in the same way that *lily* in several Oriental languages specifies simply a dainty flower.

In addition to this use as a detergent, the leaves and roots were also used as a remedy for scrofula and skin diseases in general. The chemical concerned is saponin, and the lather has been recommended for restoring ancient and delicate fabrics and old taspestries. Dried plants are placed in muslin bags, then boiled in distilled water, the solution being used cold.

The fragrant pink or white flowers bloom throughout the summer and are especially fragrant at night. They are frequently visited by sphinx moths and, in late afternoon, hawkmoths, the latter often mistaken for hummingbirds.

The plants are spreaders and can adapt to many soil conditions but need full sun. They are valuable in both the wild garden and the border and can be used to carpet a bank.

Goutweed *(Aegopodium podagraria)* is a rampant weed. This plant was once used to relieve the pains of gout, a complaint fairly common among the church hierarchy, hence its other common name, bishopweed. History and rumor both suggest that many of the highest clerics lived well. *Aegopodium* stems from the Greek *aix,* "goat," and *pod-,* "foot," from a supposed similarity of the leaf form. *Podagraria* means a cure for gout.

But there is a variegated form that is sold by most nurseries and, though still wild, is more restrained because it has traded some of its chlorophyll for the white areas. This particular form is fine for holding banks where nothing else will grow or for naturalizing in an open woodland that needs an understory that is completely self-sufficient.

And so what's in a name? That which we call a rose by any other name would smell as sweet. But would it? I really don't know. Yet when the name of a flower is a part of history, somehow the flower deserves more than just a passing glance.

As Edward FitzGerald in the *Rubáiyát of Omar Khayyám* wrote,

> *I sometimes think that never blows so red*
> *The Rose as where some buried Caesar bled—*

Snowy-Day
Diversions

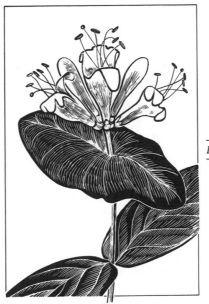

Wild honeysuckle   *Lonicera dioica*

I've never tallied the poems written to honor wildflowers. Considering the number of quotes found in luncheon programs provided for the various conservation, wildflower, and garden societies—not to mention the efforts of the so-called serious poets—the amount must be staggering. And I also will stick out my neck and say that more of those poems are written in the American dialect than in any other tongue.

In colonial times, even the wilder regions of Europe and England were more civilized than most of America. Europeans were having teas beneath crystal chandeliers while the majority of the early American settlers were wondering what horrors the next winter would bring. America has always been partly wild, and that wild part of America is evident in its poetry. Take these lines from Byron in "Hymn of Pan,"

> *The wind in the reeds and the rushes,*
> *The bees on the bells of thyme—*

or Wordsworth in "Lines Written in Early Spring,"

> *Through primrose tufts, in that sweet bower,*
> *The periwinkle trailed its wreaths—*

and compare them with the first lines of Freneau's "The Wild Honeysuckle":

> *Fair flower, that dost so comely grow,*
> *Hid in this silent, dull retreat—*

I cannot imagine an English poet using the word *dull* in such a manner, and it makes a combination of words that once read is hard to forget.

Obviously, there are many more poems devoted to wild-flowers than the following selections. But I think these represent a fairly complete sampling of the last two hundred years.

The first true American poet was Philip Freneau (1752–1832). He was born in New York City. A 1771 graduate of Princeton, he was a classmate of James Madison. Freneau was the country's first professional journalist and a powerful supporter of the American Revolution. While serving as a privateer, he was captured and then imprisoned on the brig *Aurora*. His poem "The British Prison Ship" was a direct result of the trials faced by prisoners on that ship.

A resident of New Jersey, Freneau wrote many political and satirical poems that have now gone to rest. But his position as the first important American lyric poet is respected, and much of his reputation is based on poems like "The Wild Honeysuckle" and "The Indian Burying Ground."

He was found dead in his eighty-first year in the middle of a swamp meadow—the result of going to see his garden in a snowstorm.

I suspect that today he is rolling over in his New Jersey grave after the centuries of change brought to the Garden State, including the swamps filled with rusted cars and trucks and the miles of superhighways that leap over once beautiful meadows and wetlands. His thoughts in "The Wild Honeysuckle" hold dark forebodings of things to come:

Fair flower, that dost so comely grow,
  Hid in this silent, dull retreat,
Untouched thy honied blossoms blow,
  Unseen thy little branches greet:
    No roving foot shall crush thee here,
    No busy hand provoke a tear.

By Nature's self in white arrayed,
  She bade thee shun thy vulgar eye,
And planted here the guardian shade,
  And sent soft water murmuring by;
    Thus quietly thy summer goes,
    Thy days declining to repose.

Smit with those charms, that must decay,
  I grieve to see your future doom;
They died—nor were those flower more gay,
  The flower that did in Eden bloom;
    Unpitying frosts and Autumn's power
    Shall leave no vestige of this flower.

From morning suns and evening dews
At first thy little being came;
If nothing once, you nothing lose,
For when you die you are the same;
The space between is but an hour,
The frail duration of a flower.

William Cullen Bryant (1794–1878) wrote a great deal of nature poetry before he was twenty-one, his age when admitted to the bar after a year of study at Williams College. Following ten years of practicing law in Great Barrington, Massachusetts, he left for New York City where his reputation as a poet was secure, especially because of "Thanatopsis," blank verse written when he was sixteen years old in which Nature discusses death:

Old oceans gray and melancholy waste, –
Are but the solemn decorations all
Of the great tomb of man. – "

He went to work in 1826 as an editor at the *New York Evening Post,* and from 1829 until his death he was editor-in-chief. His paper was famous for its correct applications of English. It was a leading journal of free trade and had anti-slavery leanings. His poem "The Death of the Flowers" takes the melancholia of autumn to, I fear, unscalable heights, and in this century, when we enjoy the comforts of central heating, it is a bit much:

The wind-flower and the violet, they perished long ago,
And the brier-rose and the orchid died amid the summer
* glow –*
The south wind searches for the flowers whose fragrance
* late he bore,*
And sighs to find them in the wood and by the stream no
* more.*

Some American garden writers have talked about the English penchant for sadness in the season of fall, but these poets of a season's sadness are often outdone by their American counterparts. Bryant's style did not fail in his poem "To the Fringed Gentian," to wit:

Thou waitest late, and com'st alone
When woods are bare and birds have flown,
And frosts and shortening days portend
The aged year is near his end.

Bryant wrote more cheerful stuff when his muse left the confines of Manhattan. "The Prairies," for example, is a bit brighter in tone:

These are the gardens of the Desert, these
The unshorn fields, boundless and beautiful,
For which the speech of England has no name —

But Ralph Waldo Emerson (1803–1882), the son of a Unitarian minister, experienced many sad happenings in his life and a wedding to the metaphysical transcendentalists before he could write the following poem, entitled "Musketaquid":

All my hurts
My garden spade can heal. A woodland walk,
A quest of river-grapes, a mocking thrush,
A wild rose or rock-loving columbine,
Salve my worst wounds.

Or this stanza from "My Garden":

In my plot no tulips blow, —
Snow-loving pines and oaks instead;

And rank the savage maples grow
From Spring's faint flush to Autumn red.

John Greenleaf Whittier (1807–1892) was a Quaker who received a scanty education. But he was a voracious reader and in 1857 he began contributing to the newly founded *Atlantic Monthly*. His poem to childhood, "The Barefoot Boy," gave him popularity second only to Longfellow. People would sit before the fire and entertain themselves by reading "Snow-Bound," just as later they would sit in front of the radio. (Today's TV, of course, wants no "talking heads" but rather insists that everything move, as in the movies.) "Fools, Knaves—Flowers and Trees" is short and says it all:

Give fools their gold, and knaves their power;
Let fortune's bubbles rise and fall;
Who sows a field, or trains a flower,
Or plants a tree, is more than all.

Henry Wadsworth Longfellow (1807–1882) was first and foremost a national figure, but his work was read all over the civilized world. "The Wreck of the Hesperus," "The Village Blacksmith," and the epic "The Song of Hiawatha" were as popular then as Jackie Collins's novels are today. The second stanza of "Aftermath" is about flowers but seems to hearken back fifty years to the sorrow of winters in the Harvard area:

Not the sweet, new grass with flowers
Is this harvesting of ours;
Not the upland clover bloom;
But the rowen mixed with weeds,
Tangled tufts from marsh and meads,
Where the poppy drops its seeds
In the silence and the gloom.

Jones Very (1813–1880) also wrote a number of poems dedicated to nature. He was a friend to Emerson and Thoreau and a contributor to *The Dial*, the journal of the transcendentalists. Like the others of that group, he wrote poetry that once again has the moody quality born of short summers and long winters. "The Columbine" mourns the passing of time; "The Sumach Leaves" does the same but paints the New England autumn as a time of color, if not joy:

Some autumn leaves a painter took,
  And with his colors caught their hues;
So true to nature did they look
  That none to praise them could refuse.

The yellow mingling with the red
  Shone beauteous in their bright decay,
And round a golden radiance shed,
  Like that which hangs o'er parting day.

Their sister leaves, that, fair as these,
  Thus far had shared a common lot,
All soiled and scattered by the breeze
  Are now by every one forgot.

Soon, trodden under foot of men,
  Their very forms will cease to be,
Nor they remembered be again,
  Till Autumn decks once more the tree.

But these shall still their beauty boast,
  To praise the painter's wondrous art,
When Autumn's glories all are lost
  And with the fading year depart;

And through the wintry months so pale
  The sumach's brilliant hues recall;

Where, waving over hill and vale,
  They gave its splendor to our fall.

Emily Dickinson (1830–1886) had a unique command of the English language. Her poems, rather than being interpretations of nature, become Nature herself with all her conflicts and inconsistencies. "As If Some Little Arctic Flower" is such a poem:

As if some little Arctic flower
Upon the polar hem—
Went wandering down the Latitudes
Until it puzzled came
To continents of summer—
To firmaments of sun—
To strange, bright crowds of flowers—
And birds, of foreign tongue!
I say, As if this little flower
To Eden, wandered in—
What then? Why nothing,
Only, your inference therefrom!

Not until Lizette Woodworth Reese (1856–1935), a poet from Baltimore, do we find another well-known poem dedicated to a wildflower. "A Flower of Mullein" has these lines:

I am too near, too clear a thing for you,
A flower of mullein in a crack of wall,
The villagers half see, or not at all;
Part of the weather, like the wind or dew.

Then Frank Dempster Sherman (1860–1916) wrote "A Hollyhock":

Seraglio of the Sultan Bee!
I listen at the waxen door,
And hear the zithern's melody
And sound of dancing on the floor.

Robert Loveman (1864–1923) was a southern poet. His "April Rain" should be familiar to all:

It isn't raining rain to me,
It's raining daffodils;
In every dimpled drop I see
Wild flowers on the hills.

The clouds of gray engulf the day
And overwhelm the town;
It isn't raining rain to me,
It's raining roses down.

It isn't raining rain to me,
But fields of clover bloom,
Where any buccaneering bee
Can find a bed and room.

A health unto the happy,
A fig for him who frets!
It isn't raining rain to me,
It's raining violets.

H. L. Mencken is reputed to have said that this poem was used as an excuse for "much verse that demands the sacrifice of trees to publish." I continue to wonder about "April Showers," as written by Silvers and DeSylva and sung by Larry Parks playing Al Jolson in *The Jolson Story* (1946).

Arthur Guiterman (1872–1943) was born in Vienna of American parents and was best known for humorous verse as well as for being the librettist for an opera by Walter Damrosch, *A Man Without a Country*, produced in New York in 1937. He was the past president of the Poetry Society of America. Although "Columbines" is not in the vein of Ogden Nash, it has its lighter side:

Late were we sleeping
  Deep in the mold,
Clasping and keeping
  Yesterday's gold—
Hoardings of sunshine,
  Crimson and gold;
Dreaming of light till our dream became
Aureate bells and beakers of flame,—
Splashed with the splendor of wine, of flame.
  Raindrop awoke us;
  Zephyr bespoke us;
  Chick-a-dee called us,
  Bobolink called us,—
    Then we came.

Margaret Widdemer (1897–1978) was a poet and novelist from Doylestown, Pennsylvania. Her poems include "The Factories," about child labor, and the novel "The Rose Garden Husband." Here is the first and third stanza of "The Faithless Flowers":

I went this morning down to where the Johnny-Jump-
  Ups grow
Like naughty purple faces nodding in a row.
I stayed 'most all the morning there—I sat down on a
  stump
And watched and watched and watched them—and they
  never gave a jump!

*And then the Bouncing Bets don't bounce—I tried them
  yesterday,
I picked a big pink bunch down in the meadow where
  they stay,
I took a piece of string I had and tied them in a ball,
And threw them down as hard as hard—they never
  bounced at all!*

Wildflower poetry again hit a high in Dorothy Parker (1893–1967). Miss Parker was best known as a member of the Algonquin Round Table and a writer of sardonic light verse. With "The Evening Primrose" we reach the end of a circle that began with that wild honeysuckle of the 1700s:

*You know the bloom, unearthly white,
That none has seen by morning light—
  The gentle moon, alone, may bare
  It's beauty to the secret air.
Who ventures past its dark retreat
Must kneel for holy things and sweet.
  That blossom, mystically blown,
  No man may gather for his own
Nor touch it, lest it droop and fall. . . .
Oh, I am not like that at all!*

SOURCES FOR PLANTS

The following nurseries sell seeds, plants, or both. Most of them charge for catalogs, so it's advisable to send a query postcard if you are unsure about costs.

SEEDS

Chiltern Seeds, Bortree Stile, Ulverston, Cumbria, Canada LA12 7PB. A large collection of wildflowers.

Far North Gardens, 16785 Harrison, Livonia, MI 48154. Rare and unusual seeds, including many native plants.

The Fragrant Path, Box 328, Fort Calhoun, NE 68023. Many interesting fragrant plants.

J. L. Hudson, Seedsman, P.O. Box 1058, Redwood City, CA 94064. Huge selection of seeds.

The Seed Source, Balsam Grove, NC 28708. Many unusual seeds, including a large selection of native plants.

Moon Mountain Wildflowers, P.O. Box 34, Morro Bay, CA 93442. Native American seeds.

Plants of the Southwest, 1570 Pacheco Street, Santa Fe, NM 87501. Wildflowers and grasses.

Clyde Robin Seed Company, P.O. Box 2855, Castro Valley, CA 94546. American wildflower seeds.

PLANTS

Forestfarm, 990 Tethercow Road, Williams, OR 97544. Wide selection of plants, including many rare native Americans.

Holbrook Farm and Nursery, Route 2, Box 223B, Fletcher, NC 28732. Common and rare plants, including wildflowers and ferns.

Niche Gardens, 1111 Dawson Road, Chapel Hill, NC 27516. Wildflowers galore; all propagated at the nursery.

The Primrose Path, R.D. 2, Box 110, Scottsdale, PA 15683. Ferns and native American plants.

Prairie Nursery, P.O. Box 365, Westfield, WI 53964. American grasses and wildflowers.

Rocknoll Nursery, 9210 U.S. 50, Hillsboro, OH 45133. Rock garden plants and perennials.

Sandy Mush Herbs, Route 2, Surrett Cove Road, Leicester, NC 28748. Herbs and perennials.

Sunlight Gardens, Route 1, Box 600-A, Hillvale Road, Andersonville, TN 37705. Wildflowers and ferns of eastern North America.

We-Du Nurseries, Route 5, Box 724, Marion, NC 28752. Many unusual American wildflowers.

Woodlanders, 1128 Colleton Avenue, Aiken, SC 29801. Many fine wildflowers, native trees, and shrubs.

INDEX

Index

Index

Plantago major, 36
Pleasence, Donald, 70
Plotkin, Mark J., 139
Pokeweed, see *Phytolacca americana*
Polygala paucifolia, **49**, 49-51
  sanguinea, 50
  senega, 50
  viridescens, 50
Polyploidy, definition of, 210
Polystichum acrostichoides, 57
Polytrichum commune, **18**, 153-54
Pond, planting a, 31-34
Populus tremuloides, 176
Potter, Beatrix, 20
Potter's New Cyclopaedia, 139, 142, 186
Poverty grass, see *Danthonia spicata*
Practical Encyclopedia of Gardening, The, 114
Prenanthes alba, 140
Price, Vincent, 88
Primula officinalis, 32
Prinos verticillatus, 217
Propertius's dusky wing, 91
Protonema, definition of, 150
Pteridium aquilinum, 53
Pterospora spp., 123
Pupa, 92
Purple coneflower, see *Echinacea purpurea*
Purple loosestrife, see *Lythrum salicaria*

Quackgrass, see *Agropyron repens*
Quaking aspen, see *Populus tremuloides*
Quercus ilex, 217

Ragweed, see *Ambrosia* spp.
Ranchipur, 2, 25
Rattlesnake plantain, see *Goodyera repens*
Rauvolfia serpentina, 139
Red admiral butterfly, 96
Redouté, Pierre-Joseph, 100
Reed, Chester A., 149
Reese, Lizette Woodworth, 238
Reindeer moss, see *Cladonia rangiferina*
Rhus typhina, 174-75
  'Laciniata', **173**
Robert, Duke of Normandy, 67
Robinson, William, 101, 113, 116, 165, 213
Rock cotoneaster, see

Cotoneaster horizontalis
Rock lichen, see *Lecidea speirea*
Rogers, Julia Ellen, 177
Rombauer, Irma, 62
Rosa multiflora, 221
Royal fern, see *Osmunda regalis* var. *spectabilis*
Royal Horticultural Dictionary of Gardening, 171
Rubaiyat of Omar Khayyam, 230
Rudbeckia hirta, 4
  'Gloriosa', 210
Rumex acetosa, **60**, 60-63
  acetosella, 62

St. Apollonia of dentistry, 204
St. Barbara of Heliopolis, 203
St. Fiacre, **203**, 204-7
St. Robert, 67
Salix alba, 140
Salticus scenicus, 133-34
Sanguinaria canadensis, 4, **28**, 28-30
  'Multiplex', 30
Saponaria ocymoides, 149
  officinalis, 229
Saprophyte, definition of, 118
Sargent, Professor, 44
Sarracenia purpurea, **78**, 80, 81-82
Sarrazin, Dr. Michel, 81
Schimper, William Philipp, 154
Schizachyrium scoparium, 223
Sedum 'Autumn Joy', 222
Seneca snakeroot, see *Polygala senega*
Sensitive fern, see *Onoclea sensibilis*
Serrate, definition of, 114
Shakespeare, 92
Shasta daisy, 227
Sheep sorrel, see *Rumex acetosella*
Short, Dr. Charles W., 43
Shortia galacifolia, **42**, 42-44
Short-stalked damselfly, 89
Showy ladyslipper, see *Cypripedium reginae*
Siberian dogwood, see *Cornus alba* 'Siberica'
Side-oats grama, see *Bouteloua curtipendula*
Sieveking, Albert Forbes, 204
Sikes, Bill, 117
Silver spotted skipper, 96
Simulium spp., **25**, 25-27
Skippers, 87
Skunk cabbage, see *Symplocarpus foetidus*

Slugs, 27, **105**, 105-9
Smith, James Edward, 198
Solidago altissima, 192
  canadensis, 192
  'Cloth of Gold', 193
  'Crown of Rays', 193
  'Gold Dwarf', 193
  'Minuta', 193
  nemoralis, 192
  odora, **191**, 191-93
Sorghastrum avenaceum, 182
Sorrel, see *Rumex acetosa*
Spadix, 39
Spadix, definition of, 12
Spartina pectinata, 181
Spathe, definition of, 12
Spider, ballooning of, 127
Spider mites, life cycle of, 110-11
Spiders, 126-37
Spider web, construction of, 128-29, **129**
Spinoza, 125
Spleenwort, ebony, see *Asplenium platyneuron*
Spleenwort, see *Asplenium platyneuron*
Sporophyte, 150
Spotted coralroot, see *Corallorhiza maculata*
Spring azure butterfly, 94
Squawroot, see *Conopholis* spp.
Stachys byzantina, 222
Staghorn sumac, see *Rhus typhina*
Stem mothers, 109
Steyermark, Julian A., 116
Stiles, Mr., 44
Stone-loving andreaea, see *Andreaea petrophila*
Stoneroot, 186
Strawberry tree, see *Arbutus unedo*
Summer Cooking, 61
Sundew, see *Drosera* spp.
Sundrops, see *Oenothera fruticosa* or *O. tetragona*
Swain, Ralph, 103
Swallowtail butterfly, 96
Sweet, Robert, 65
Sweet fern, see *Comptonia peregrina*
Switch grass, see *Panicum virgatum*
Symplocarpus foetidus, **10**, 10-13

Taettemaelk or ropy milk, 83
Tale of Two Cities, A, 207